Signs of
CONTACT

TRIGUEIRINHO

Signs of
CONTACT

*The bold account of the experience
of transcending death*

Shasti Association

Copyright © 1989 Jose Trigueirinho Netto

The profits generated from sales of books by Trigueirinho are used for the maintenance of spiritual centers.

Original Title in Portuguese:

SINAIS DE CONTATO – Sao Paulo, Brazil: Editora Pensamento.
Copyright © 1989 by José Trigueirinho Netto

Cover photo by author

Cataloging-in-Publication data

Trigueririnho Netto, José
Signs of Contact: The bold account of the experience of transcending death.
Trigueirinho. – Mount Shasta, CA, Shasti Association 2nd edition, 2020
150 p.
ISBN: 978-1-948430-00-5
Library of Congress Control Number: 2017945326
1. Occult science
2. Subterranean civilizations
3. Spiritual life.
I. Title.
DDC: 10-05157

English language rights reserved

Shasti Association
P.O. Box 318
Mt. Shasta, CA 96067-0318
editorial@shasti.org
www.shasti.org

*Since time immemorial
humanity of the surface of the Earth
has tried to transcend death.
Now, the time to do this has arrived.*

Contents

Publisher's Introduction   i

Part One
COMING TO THE VALLEY

What is incomplete will be completed	3
The open air: the pyramid of today	31
The leap in the dark	47

Part Two
THE NIGHT OF ERKS

The first night	67
The night of the baptism	81
Three weeks later	91
Phases of purification	105

Part Three
THE NEW LIFE

Taking on the new contacts	119
The three requests	129
To participate in the intergalactic journey	141

APPENDIX

The law of transmutation	147
Cleansing the stables	157
About Trigueirinho and His Work	165
Books by Trigueirinho	169

Publisher's Introduction

Is there a soul? Can it exist independently of the body and leave and re-enter it? What remains of the personality after physical death? All of the great religious and spiritual traditions of the world attempt to answer these and related questions. Another question we might also ask is if the higher being of a person can offer its body to be used by another, more advanced being, for a spiritual purpose.

This latter phenomenon, called "transmutation," has been discussed in the occult literature by Blavatsky, Steiner and other writers, is the subject of "The Idyll of the White Lotus" (a theosophical novel) and has been described in numerous autobiographical testimonies. Thoughtful answers to all of these questions are provided in this book, Signs of Contact, which is a personal report of the author's own transmutation experience. Signs of Contact addresses many important topics of interest to spiritual seekers, including the nature of the student-teacher relationship, the deeper meaning of surrender, the possibility and nature of human contact with beings from other dimensions, the meaning of spiritual service and its scope of operation, and much more.

What is unusual about this book is the phenomenological approach that it takes. Rather than offer theories, explanations, or arguments for spiritual phenomenon, the author simply describes his own experience – articulately, knowledgably, and in detail – that took place in the "Valley of ERKS", a sacred energetic center in the mountains of Argentina, under the guidance of an advanced spiritual teacher. Here we see described in scientific detail the experience of a mature soul who is open to contact with subtle realms, whose understanding of spiritual service is planetary and cosmic rather than merely individual, and who has prepared – over the course of many incarnations – to surrender his lower bodies to be used in service of a divine plan, and who is willing and able, with the expert guidance of a teacher, to allow them to be used for a higher purpose.

Trigueirinho generously offers his own experience to help us re-interpret and re-present many ancient spiritual practices and tenets in a form that is suitable to the needs of modern spiritual seekers, explaining why these old forms may no longer serve us and showing us how their essence can be preserved and expressed in new forms. He explains, for example, how the formal rituals and practices associated with initiation as described in ancient texts, are no longer necessary or suitable. In our times initiation may occur as an inner experience, free from outer ritual and form, as was the author's own experience of initiation in the Valley of ERKS.

Signs of Contact concludes with an excerpt from the author's book on the Hercules myth: "A Time for Inner Growth: The Myth of Hercules Today"* offering us a deep symbolic spiritual analyses of Hercules experience of "Cleansing the Stables" – one that we can apply to our own lives and spiritual transformation as we ourselves face this inner cleansing task, and finally, a chapter on the different kinds of transmutation.

These writings demonstrate his remarkable ability to reframe and re-interpret ancient spiritual truths and to place them in a contemporary form while also addressing issues not usually discussed in spiritual teachings, such as: our relationship to the environment, and the mineral, animal and vegetable kingdoms; the negative karmic burden that we carry from the history of slavery and the genocide of indigenous peoples; and the nature of spiritual work in groups, for example. He also addresses issues of healing, a larger vision of astrology, the esoteric nature of symbols, sound and colors, the divine feminine, the emerging "New Humanity" and its "Communities-of-Light."

Signs of Contact, along with his other books is a goldmine of information on these and other topics.

In summary, there is much to learn in this book for those of us who are interested in these topics, whether or not we personally accept the possibility of transmutation itself.

*Originally published in Portuguese by Editora Pensamento, Sao Paulo, Brazil with the title *Hora De Crescer Interiormente: O Mito de Hércules Hoje* and also in Spanish by Editoral Kier, Buenos Aires, Argentina as *Hora de Crecer Interiormente: El Mito de Hércules, Hoy*.

Part One

Coming to the Valley

*"If the sky were no longer pure,
it would soon be dissolved"*

What is incomplete will be completed

At the hour of twilight, we set out for the Valley of ERKS, an area of contact with cosmic visitors who for millions of years, have been coming to the Earth. We were driving along the roads of the province of Cordoba, in Argentina, toward that mountainous region that had formerly been the bottom of an ocean. On the rock formations that surrounded us, we saw marks of erosion, an ancient work of the sea water. The mountains, that radiated their own energy and that of the minerals, had sculpted in them human faces, heads or bodies of animals, and also other symbolic forms. Although there were no flowers on this road or nearby either, as we approached the area, a scent of geranium was noticed more and more intensely inside the vehicle. As soon as the scent became perceptible, I knew that it indicated the presence of cosmic beings. As we realized this we saw in the sky, on our right, a space vessel that looked like a bright star. Much closer than a real star, its brightness increased and decreased, giving us sign of its collaboration with the work that would begin there with us.

Many of the bright points that exist in the celestial sphere are neither stars nor planets, but extraterrestrial or intraterrestrial vessels carrying out tasks. There are individuals who learn to identify them; they get to contact them inwardly and obtain replies from them. The famous *Star of Bethlehem*, for example, mentioned in the Bible, was in reality a vessel doing a sacred work, in a moment especially meaningful for the evolution of the Earth.

The car continued through the mountains, going up a little road bordered by vegetation that had been burned by a fire lit by people still far from knowing how to coexist with Nature and respect life. The scent of geranium remained with us, and space vessels continued to accompany us.

Now we could see others, besides the one that had appeared in the beginning of the way. They announced that in a little while there would be a great operation, in order that we make contact with a sector of the work performed by cosmic races for the planet.

Whenever the Earth is close to a transition, the presence of these space vessels becomes visible. It was so in the time of Atlantis, as is mentioned in the Bible and as is also happening today. The intense work done by them shows that we are close to the time for an operation of global scale. We continued, however, toward these contacts, without creating expectations or nourishing in ourselves any interest in sensationalism or phenomena, heading towards an encounter with the unknown with a simple attitude, without fear, enthusiasm or emotions. And, in this atmosphere of inner and outer tranquility, transformations began to happen.

Rapid progress is occurring in the consciousness of some individuals. To be able to keep unusually calm and impartial before issues that, at other times, would have stirred up emotions demonstrates this fact. H owever, far from being an indifference, this new state of mind corresponds to a getting close to that which is real because, in truth, it is only possible to deeply understand a fact or an inner situation when we are impartial about them. It was in this spirit that I remained calm before the unusual realities I had to face, as if they were absolutely normal to the senses. This account may help other individuals accept with wisdom the detachment they presently experience.

In the wide horizon around us, we saw the harmonious activity of vessels whose lights turned on and off. A kind of subtle, intangible communication took place between us; and they presented themselves to us as if they were old acquaintances. Some slid across the physical space only a few inches off the ground, silently crossing the valley, moving to the left until they stopped at specific spots where they would send out more intense signals, as the luminous nuclei that they are. These signals obey a code of their own, and the pauses are part of the work of recognition in connecting with other vessels. The range of action of these vessels is very wide; transcending the place in which they manifest themselves and, often, even the limits of this solar system. On our extreme right, at the point where this operation began, a large, brilliant vessel of orange-yellow light, commanded these sacred maneuvers. Meanwhile, other smaller ones disappeared into the interior of the mountains and into the subterranean layers of the soil. When coming across a physical obstacle in its way, an extraterrestrial or intraterrestrial vessel can instantly change dimensions, entering into supraphysical levels. It has the capacity of going through any material body without creating impact or friction. This is one of the reasons why so many space vessels can move harmoniously within the orbit of the Earth in this period. The other reasons are of a subtler order, for communication between more highly evolved beings is internal, and therefore, infallible when taking place on stable vibratory planes. There have been reports of accidents in this field, all of them caused by the recklessness or ignorance of pilots and terrestrial astronauts who entered the magnetic field of a materialized space vessel.[1]

From the location where I encountered them, I could not see the place where the vessels entered the mountains, but I perceived that their disappearance was orderly. The whole operation was like a symphony led by an experienced cosmic conductor, a representative of the Order of the Universes. While we were there, we witnessed more than a hundred vessels return from different missions to various points of the Earth. We had no information about the tasks they performed, but the vessels allowed us to perceive them, indicating that everything was controlled by a sidereal engineering, if such a term could be applied to these cases of extreme order and supraphysical

---

[1] Scientific records contain reports about such incidents

organization. Expressing a subtle communication code, they brightened and dimmed their light, allowing us to even take photographs at certain moments. Without resorting to special technical devices, it was possible to register realities existing on supraphysical levels, because the vessels would send a vibratory wave to the camera and the film, to signal as a sign of consent. Events like these are becoming more and more common, as will be seen in the near future.

During the times to come, the telluric, atmospheric, magnetic and spiritual conditions of the terrestrial orbit will require more and more assistance from beings capable of understanding the laws of super-nature and therefore, to help life on the surface of the Earth restore its equilibrium, which has been significantly altered, mainly in the last decades.

The degree of loss of ozone in the atmosphere and the heating of the planet alone would constitute an imminent global crisis. Tons of gases such as chloro-fluoro-carbon (CFC)are poured into the terrestrial atmosphere by industries and by the inhabitants of cities each year. This gas is normally used in refrigerators, industrial solvents and in other products. Such practice, which continues despite all warnings, is irreversibly altering the capacity the atmosphere has to preserve life.

The contribution that numerous intergalactic space vessels bring to the planet by transmuting the poisoning that it is presently victim of is inestimable and largely unknown. Although such contribution is limited by human free will, which is respected as long as humanity does not alter the equilibrium of extraterrestrial space, immense benefits come from this continuous activity in Earth's orbit.

CFC destroys the ozone layer of the planet, absorbing the heat radiating from the ground and carrying it to the atmosphere. As a consequence of this increase in the planet's temperature, polar ice tends to melt, bringing about significant alterations in the level of the sea and contributing to the process of global warming. "Global warming is inevitable and it is only a matter of time", the National Aeronautics and Space Administration of the United States assures us.

Thus, the entrance of salt water into the continents' current sources of irrigation water is inevitable, to result in many areas remaining without potable water and flooding almost all the coastal region. With an increase in temperature of only two degrees, hurricanes become more frequent and much more violent; with an increase of seven degrees, arable areas become arid and sterile.

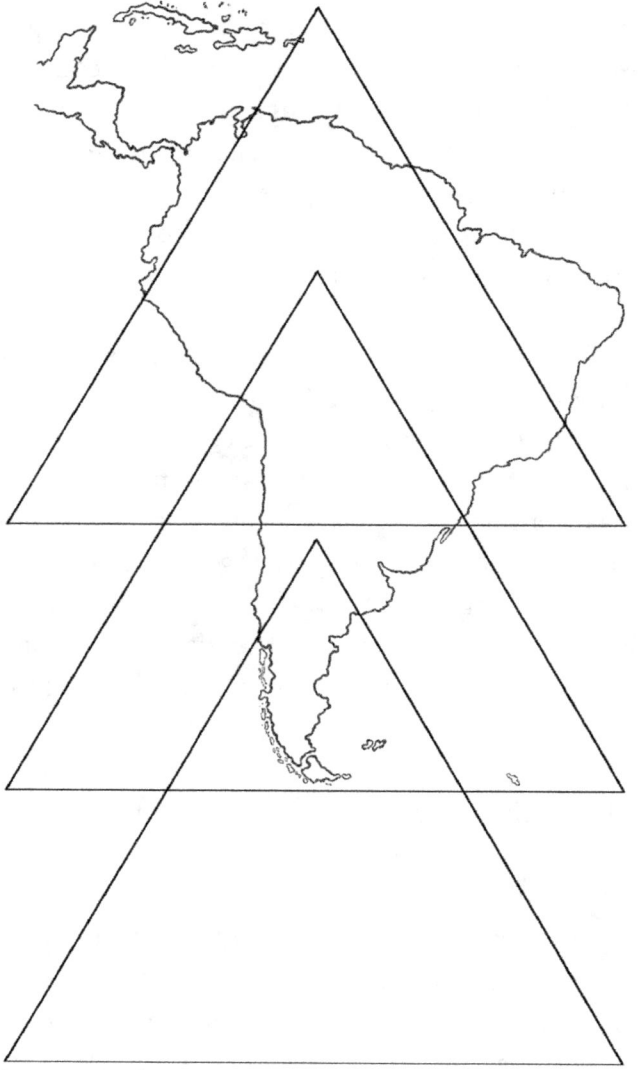
Energy triangles integrated into the ono-zone field of energy.

However, these are the scientific projections that do not incorporate broader perceptions. In reality, while this is happening through the indifference of political and economic governments of the Earth's surface, the planet's magnetic axis is preparing to incline. For this reason, it will be necessary for intergalactic space vessels to perform special operations to purify the magnetism of the planet and transport – which they are already doing – beings from the mineral, plant, animal and human kingdoms to subtle levels of life, to concrete levels of other planets and even to the inner part of the Earth, which will pass through a period of balancing and regeneration. This subject has been treated in more detail in the book MIZ TLI TLAN – *A World that Awakens*.[2]

Great triangles of energy were established in South America also, to make terrestrial magnetism more subtle-like inter-communicating pyramids integrated into the universal Ono-Zone[3] energy field and acting according to the law of purification, as we have explained in the book MIZ TLI TLAN. The first triangle refers to this important intraterrestrial center and covers the central region of the continent, Brazil and part of Argentina; the second is linked to

---

[2] See also NISKALKAT (A Message for Times of Emergency).by Trigueirinho, Editora Pensamento, Sao Paulo, Brazil

[3] Ono-Zone: creative energy that supports the existence of the cosmos, in its various levels of manifestation.

the activity of ERKS and is made up of parts of Brazil, Chile, Uruguay, Paraguay and Argentina; the third triangle is concerned with the work of the Iberah center,[4] and is formed by the south of Argentina, part of Chile, Uruguay, and the Antarctic territory.

These triangles of energy form part of an intergalactic operation to elevate terrestrial life, an operation that has South America as one of its principal bases on Earth. They give a brief idea of how much humanity inhabiting the surface of the planet is assisted by superior forces, despite their unconsciousness of the energy network that in reality preserves it.

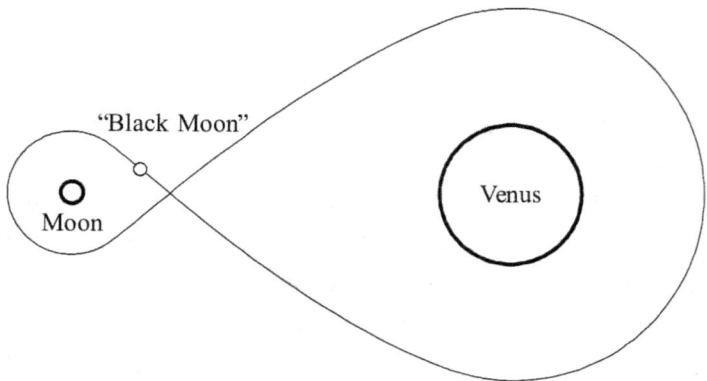

Pathway of the artificial satellite around the Moon.

Extra-planetary energies assist terrestrial science to accomplish tasks that are still unreachable for it.

---

[4] See UNVEILED SECRETS (Iberah and Anu Tea)

According to a well-known contact-person,[5] science is aware of the existence of an artificial satellite, commanded by extraterrestrial civilizations, that makes its way between the Moon and Venus, in a continuous and uninterrupted rhythm.

The objective of this permanent operation is to keep the Moon in its orbit, preventing it from getting too close to the Earth and in this way, avoiding the possibility of a shock. This same contact-person has stated that he was in this satellite, called "Black Moon", and that its trajectory describes a very characteristic course for those who know it.

According to his information, in the interior of the Black Moon he found bodies of extraterrestrial beings in a state of "unfoldment", that is, beings who leave their denser bodies in the satellite while, in consciousness or in subtle bodies, they render service on Earth. For these extraterrestrial beings, this controlled unfolding is the same as sleep is for us.

It was affirmed that there are millions of beings from space working on Earth under these conditions. There are terrestrial human beings, advanced in consciousness, who also work during their physical sleep.

---

[5] Contact-person: a being who has a direct and conscious relationship with evolved extraterrestrial or intraterrestrial civilizations, a process that is generally mediated by space vessels and by the Hierarchies present in them.

We have referred to them in the book OUR LIFE IN DREAMS.[6]

As regards the maneuvers and preparation for the operations already mentioned, we perceived that they are intelligent and harmonious, and developed by groups of vessels with different potentials. Thus, the whole planet finds itself demarcated and receives permanent assistance to be able to go through this important phase of transition.

Our account is concerned with ERKS, with the great intraterrestrial center situated in the supraphysical region of Cordoba (Argentina), inhabited by beings from different parts of the cosmos.

The work done by this center was described from a more philosophical point of view in the book ERKS-*Inner World*.[7] We propose to examine new aspects here.

The Valley of ERKS, a region that on the surface of the planet focuses the work of this center, is also called YKI SHAMUAIKA ("the chosen place," in the language Irdin.)[8]

---

[6] See also THE VISITOR *(The Way to Anu Tea)*.

[7] By the same author, Editora Pensamento.

[8] Irdin: intergalactic language, basis of all the languages spoken on Earth.

Within the energetic dome of ERKS are developed important activities for the regeneration of life on Earth, activities that are not physically visible, except when their agents become materialized or send some reflex of their existence to the physical plane of the surface.

Valley of Escoba

Ravine of the Moon

YKI

SHAMUAIKA

(the chosen place)

Mountain of Pajarito

Hill of Terrones

Hill of Uritorco

Chapel of the Hill

Grotto of Ongamira

Our contact with the center ERKS is the reason for the existence of this book, which we publish with the permission of the Commands and of the representatives of the cosmic civilizations serving on Earth. In writing it, we are neither moved by personal needs nor by the intention to satisfy curiosity. We are moved, rather, by the need that many beings from the surface of the Earth have to truly love these cosmic visitors, who are willing to work in sectors we are still not prepared for, and to teach us aspects of the new planetary law that today are still unknown.

In order to participate in such a harmonious rhythm, we arrived, as was mentioned in the beginning, at the contact area during the last moments of dusk. It was summer and, therefore, it got dark much later. We reached about five thousand-six hundred feet above sea level, driving up a winding mountain road under a sky that was already starry. On the right a big rock cut by Nature in the shape of a camel seemed to guard the physical setting. Another immense rock resembled a cosmonaut, looking at the sky in the direction from which the vessels came.

Upon getting out of the car, we received a strong gust of wind - for us one more sign that the cosmic beings were there. It was a warm gale that started and ended suddenly, as a greeting. After it stopped, we turned to a big mountain and my companion sent out a great shout in that direction. The echo repeated itself eight times, each one of them representing a hierarchical group present there.

We also noticed the work the energies did in the air, on the rocks and on the earth beneath us. With the assistance of the local energies and of the waves coming from the vessels, our sight received an extra stimulation and perceived supraphysical realities. In this way we were given the possibility of seeing the waving and subtle outlines of the mountains and the gradation of the energy that was present in the entire valley, which was revealed at that height and extended for almost fifteen miles. We knew that this stimulus had a special meaning for the current times.

High in the sky was a large laboratory vessel, one of the brightest among those that made themselves visible. It looked like a star, but we could see what it really was because, around it, there were some twenty smaller vessels that slowly changed positions in a gigantic and silent ballet. In laboratory vessels such as this one, important transmuting processes take place, and terrestrial human beings can contact them and even be taken inside of them.

Until recently, negative stories about the action of the laboratory vessels were spread. Because of certain disharmonious events occurring in the past with extraterrestrial beings of less developed consciousness, human beings came to regard the presence of cosmic visitors an as interference in their affairs. However, since then, many changes have taken place in this process. The extraterrestrial beings that came to Earth to perform research in which humans of the surface were used (as is still currently done on live animals in medical schools or in scientific laboratories) have already been moved away from the planetary orbit, because they live under laws that have just been transcended here. Such negative experiences, usually reported by certain sensationalist press, took place before 8/8/88 (August 8, 1988.)[9] In other words, from this date on, the Earth began to attract the elements that correspond to its new state. The planet, now conscious of its role in cosmic space, receives more evolved beings, coming from many different universes – beings which, through service, are willing to spend long periods in space vessels, or who, even in an incorporeal state, accepted to focus their consciousness on the work of recovering the planet.

In past times, these beings of great power and love were called Archangels. Today we know that this former appearance, legendary in human culture, was a substitute for the actual presence of space vessels that may travel several light-years of distance in a few minutes under the command of these sublime beings. As in antiquity, today also, such beings defend and preserve the Earth from the action of destructive forces.

---

[9] As of August 8, 1988, the process of transition in the material levels of the Earth began, which includes the preparation for the contact with superior laws of evolution.

For long periods humans distracted themselves by their own external life, but now that the hour of great need has arrived, they turn to look at what is inside themselves - that is - to the totality of their own consciousness. The Archangels of ancient culture transmit the teaching today in the form of laws that humanity must learn, using a language that is more adequate for this age and for the new mental and spiritual states that are already announcing themselves to humanity.

The winged beings who, sword in hand, ascended and descended the immense stairways of heaven, as shown by ancient theologies, scriptures and paintings of that time, were introduced to us in a form that we could best understand and accept. The Great Fraternity[10] has always been the same; now, however, there is no longer any need to see it as so distant from us. The humans who have made a choice for inner life must be ready to know their brothers of the cosmos more close-up and, as a measure of their consciousnesses expanding, the decorative, emotional and legendary elements of inner visions and of external informational accounts will no longer be essential.

By the way, a mystic of elevated consciousness declared that she saw above her country of origin, the

---

[10] Great Fraternity: network of consciousnesses, unified by the law of love that acts on behalf of the evolution of the universes.

figure of Archangel Michael with his sword piercing a point that needed to be preserved from the disharmonizing interference of certain involutionary forces. About fifteen years earlier, this same cosmic being, who has always been known on Earth, materialized itself on the astral plane and imprinted his image on a photograph, introducing himself with the name of Ashtar Sheran. As we know, Ashtar Sheran (the Archangel Michael) presents itself whenever necessary in a powerful space vessel in the Valley of ERKS.

Was the vision of this mystic a projection of Archangel Michael himself, taking on a garment that she could understand, or was it a creation of her own Christian cultural world? It is difficult to answer this question using the human analytical mind. There are individuals who deny the existence of Archangels – but, in reality, what they really deny is the way in which the ancient scriptures presented the Celestial Hierarchies.

These individuals have not yet found the correlation between those descriptions and the ones that occur today. Between them there is only a difference of form and of degree of evolution, as much on the manifesting side as on the observing one. The apparitions of these messengers of truth are updated over the course of time, and the way of contacting humanity today is in keeping with the mental development of modern humankind. In fact, the protectors of this planet have always existed and, in this cyclic moment, it is possible to contact them more directly, according to what we saw by means of what we were allowed to experience.[11]

Regarding the experience I am narrating here, the being who was leading me to the area of ERKS and externally introducing me to this work, knew the inside of the laboratory-vessels. He explained to me that there the new genetic code could be introduced to the human being, when it is part of the plan of evolution and with the consent and collaboration of the monad[12] of the being that passes through this experience. Certain cosmic genes are then incorporated in the subtle counterpart of the pituitary gland and, from then on, the person ceases being aggressive and becomes able to function from supramental levels.

Beings whose degree of development in consciousness corresponds to that of the so-called Archangels coordinate universal dimensions. So does Ashtar Sheran. On the other hand, the laboratory vessels can be conducted by individuals of elevated knowledge, possibly known on Earth for their previous work

---

[11] See also THE BOOK OF SIGNS.

[12] Monad: nucleus of consciousness of the being at a cosmic level.

that made them famous individuals in the life of the surface. Therefore, the genetic reform that is being engendered in the human race of the surface is spiritually guided according to a divine plan of evolution, and it is carried out according to an orderly, safe and practical scheme.

Because the change of the genetic code is a controversial subject, the understanding of which is contaminated by that which presently occurs in the laboratories of the surface of the planet (a true monstrosity according to cosmic laws), various points about this were made clear to me in the course of the work. However, before sharing them, I would like to introduce the reader to the sacred atmosphere brought by the exteriorization of the Intergalactic Hierarchies that represent the evolutionary energies.

For us, up until now, the term Hierarchy referred exclusively to the spiritual government of planet Earth, since the majority of esoteric books written before 8.8.88 almost always kept silent about the other Hierarchies. Even when they were mentioned, they were kept as veiled as possible, thus following the divine orientation for the epoch. Some of them, little known to the humanity of the surface, were called "parallel hierarchies", mainly those who were active in the intergalactic or interplanetary sphere.

Today, the clear exteriorization of the space vessels brings more of an opening to demonstrate that the Intergalactic Hierarchies work in collaboration with those of the Earth, attracting to supraphysical levels the beings of this race of the surface that, until now, lived under purely material laws, without penetrating broader systems of balance and knowledge. Through these Intergalactic Hierarchies – Hierarchies of values, energies, beings, entities and groups– is expressed love-wisdom, the essential energy of this solar system, and also others, more far reaching that rule galaxies situated beyond this one where we find ourselves with our still limited consciousness. Love-wisdom is a great Ray of the infinite cosmos but, little by little, the humanity of the surface of the Earth will also learn to know the other Rays, which also have specific functions in the One and Only Work.

In the book THE ENERGY OF THE RAYS IN OUR LIVES,[13] where we address the subject of the coordination of the human personality and its harmonization with the inner animic nucleus, when presenting the seven Rays we said that "for the time being, we know little about the various Cosmic Rays that manifest themselves in other solar systems ...", and we gave the keys necessary to open the first doors to the knowledge of the infinite world of energies.

---

[13] By the same author, Editora Pensamento.

In the present book we are introducing the reader to the theme more concretely, taking him or her to the knowledge of the beings that represent the materialization of these Rays.

In the space vessels are found extraterrestrial and also intraterrestrial beings. Their function is to help us make a n ew synthesis within ourselves. These beings represent Hierarchies and each one of them expresses a Cosmic Ray. Some of these Rays manifest themselves clearly, and their spiritual and divine focal points become known; others keep themselves occult, as in the case for part of the Hierarchies of the intraterrestrial center in the Peruvian Andes, as I mentioned in the book MIZ TLI TLAN – *An Awakening World*.

From the spiritual point of view, certain intraterrestrial civilizations have reached the same level of development as some extraterrestrial ones. This is why they have always been intelligently helping the evolution of the race of the surface, where we are now incarnated. The work of the more advanced intraterrestrial beings has unified itself in this time to that of the Pleiades which fulfills the Plan of Evolution for the Earth. Pleiad is a term used to designate extraterrestrial beings originating from incorporeal regions of the cosmos, beings of a high evolutionary grade.

Therefore, regarding the degree of development, there is a difference between the humanity of the surface, still joined to the ephemeral ego, and the intraterrestrials, who have already reached certain sublime states of cosmic consciousness. From an external point of view, this difference also manifests itself because, while the former are generally conscious in the three-dimensional world only, the intraterrestrials are able to travel to different planes, taking and leaving physical bodies whenever they need to.

However, there are intraterrestrial beings that, in terms of development of consciousness, are several degrees below the humanity of the surface, and there are also extraterrestrial beings that have not yet achieved a stage of evolution that is in harmony with the universal laws controlled by the cosmic center that rules all. It is not up to us to deal with these cases here, neither with those that in antiquity were called "evil angels," nor with those who still work for involutionary forces. We are not going to deal with subjects relating to space conquest, either. The activities that are unrelated to the work of higher evolution do not concern us. We will refer only to the civilizations that cooperate with planetary evolution and with the development of the humanity of the surface, and that thus, act in consonance with the evolutionary purpose.

There are beings that live in the center of the Earth that are subordinated to other laws; they are more primitive than the human beings of the surface and follow a still more rigorous path of purification than the one followed by humankind. Djwhal Khul, the Tibetan, when he referred to these beings in his teachings, said that students should not try to contact them.

This is not, therefore, the subject of this book, and neither is the activity of extraterrestrials of inferior development. In truth, at present there are intergalactic groups that keep them within certain limits so that they do not disturb the terrestrial equilibrium, which is in a process of recovery. The space vessels that are encircling the Earth at present, working on its magnetism and balance, disintegrate any and all intrusive presences that insinuate themselves and that could interfere in its current process of transition and reconstruction.

The brothers from space that are among us, collaborate with an extensive plan of evolution, which we may know for the time being, only partially. Such Hierarchies, originating from sublime states of existence, together with the intraterrestrial beings, work on behalf of the advent of a new humanity on the surface of the Earth, one which will be in accordance with a plan established by the Councils that guide the evolution of the universes. This plan includes the incorporation of cosmic genes in humanity and the application, throughout the planet, of the law of purification. This law is put into action by superior extraterrestrial Hierarchies, connected to the Sun and even to still larger centers.

Among the extraterrestrial beings there are those who, in the past, were integrated with the intraterrestrial evolution and who transferred themselves, in due course, to divine places far from the Earth. These "places" may be called pleiades, as well as the beings that live in these conditions. These beings have exceeded the stage of humanity of the surface after having lived it on other planets and after having encountered the law of service while still in these civilizations. All these beings and civilizations are subject to the law of evolution. Each one of them, however, expresses this law in a different degree.

Some extraterrestrials maintain control over the forces of evil, that is, over the forces that are out of place in the harmonious picture of evolution. Secretly, these beings of light lead such dark forces to a manifestation that may be useful to the All.

Although the action of the forces of evil on our planet is evident, this is nothing but a passing fact, because after the imminent great purification, they will be led to other areas of the universe. Life on the surface of the Earth is going to be almost totally free from the malignant influence that today keeps its yoke on it, controlling sectors such as the circulation of money and major parts of the means of communication.

To liberate the planet from these forces is, in this end of cycle, one of the broadest missions of the extraterrestrial and intraterrestrial energies that work for the Central Celestial Government, the cosmic center of supreme intelligence. This mission has been accomplished with the cooperation of the members of the race of the surface that have chosen to render planetary service at these times.

The forces of involution, still influential on Earth today, have led humanity of the surface to insane actions, such as, for example, the fission of the atom. Fifty years have gone by since this experience was carried out for the first time, and we still continue not knowing what to do with the resulting lethal waste generated by this practice. Although some regions of the planet have been used as storage for this disintegrating residue, and because of it, have suffered with their contamination, even knowing that such residue, to not be harmful, would have to remain hermetically kept for thousands of years, the human mind was carried away by the forces of chaos to opt for this technology. In what other way can we explain the continuing use of atomic energy with full knowledge that it is deadly, and that on the material level of this planet there is no solution for the problems generated by its waste? Knowing these facts, we can clearly understand that the extraterrestrials have real reasons to be here, warning us of the worst that can happen, and protecting cosmic space from contamination. "Human beings have made too much fuss about themselves, (and) their own importance in the cosmic scale. Why shouldn't there be other forms of life superior to them, conscious intelligent beings higher in mentality, character, and spiritual knowledge, better equipped with powers and techniques?", asks the philosopher Paul Brunton in his posthumous book PERSPECTIVES.[14]

---

[14] Larson Press, Burdett, NY.

The open air: the pyramid of today

We can say that curiosity is a characteristic of consciousness polarized in the three-dimensional world, while the step of needing to know is with respect to the fulfilling of a plan of evolution and the task of each being within this plan. Therefore, when we consciously accept to collaborate with a process of purification like that which is proposed here, and when we open ourselves to new knowledge, we must remove from ourselves any and all human-emotional impulses and let ourselves be taken only by the aspiration of integrating ourselves with the new laws that will begin to rule terrestrial humanity of the surface – humanity that until now has limited itself to the planetary laws active in the material sphere, such as, for example, that of birth and of death.

In the following pages, we will deal with facts that are practically unknown on the surface of the Earth;

we will therefore be faced with unusual experiences. None of this, however, should take away from us an attitude of impartiality and neutrality – and the possibility that the light originating from a higher level will bring about greater understanding in us.

I had been invited to be physically in the Valley of ERKS, in the province of Cordoba, Argentina, six months before. Therefore, I had enough time to prepare myself for this contact. I would like to say, that during all of this period, I did my best to improve my surrender to a supraconscious plane, a plane that I felt was guiding me and leading me through paths of life in all levels – from the most concrete to those immaterial ones, often unnoticed to the human self. This improvement constituted my preparation. The certainty that I was being guided brought me a great calm, so much that I stopped perceiving the passing of time. One day, when consulting my schedule, I was surprised to see that I was already on the eve of the trip.

I knew I would live through important phases of a process of purification already taking place, and I sought to open myself unconditionally to it. Experienced beings of great wisdom collaborated in this process. Thus, without any division or doubt, I prepared myself for whatever unknowns might come, without the slightest expectation. In a certain way, I felt like those who, in the in the past, following consciously the evolutionary and supraphysical path, were ready to enter the pyramids to receive some message or inner stimulation through the elevated consciousnesses that worked there, in service to the Earth. As we know, at certain cyclical moments of the development of our being, we need intermediaries between us and the superior energies.

Words said in ancient China then came to my mind: "The spirit of the depths of the valley is imperishable." In some way, the energy that in ancient times manifested this message was present also in the valley I was heading to, a valley that would for me be like a pyramid of present times. It was sublime to experience this reality because, according to this same source of wisdom, "the Perfect Path is each moment more valuable."

I could never imagine removing myself from an experience like this, but I saw clearly, while there and available, that "the web of Heaven is infinite; that its nets are wide and from which nobody escapes". It was, therefore, inconceivable to retreat. When we arrived at the point where the valley revealed itself, we stopped the car and got out. Walking, I found myself at the edge of a precipice, but I did not look down; I looked attentively at the other extremity where a great light, the vessel that coordinated the works, would appear to give us a signal. And thus it happened. It appeared a few meters off the ground and shone on the horizon, greeting us. It was as if, commanded by a great Being, it said to me:

> *"The incomplete will be completed,*
> *The curved straightened,*
> *The empty filled,*
> *The worn out renewed,*
> *The insufficient increased,*
> *The excessive scattered."*

as was transmitted in ancient times by the TAO TE CHING.

Ceremonies like this one that was beginning in the Valley of ERKS had also occurred in the past. So today, at the end of a cycle and of a civilization, they took on another form and adapted themselves to our epoch. There were neither pyramids here, nor dark chambers, but the "ritual" was taking place in the open air, assisted by the wind, air and by the energy that displayed itself, even in the contour of the mountains, undulating and radiating themselves. All was peace and harmony, even when the strong wind blew across the area. And, when the wind died down, the sky turned completely clear. "How pure and tranquil the Path is! I do not know of whom it could be the offspring, for it seems to be prior to the Sovereign of Heaven," says the eternal wisdom.

The pleiad who accompanied me, and who was always with me in this phase of the process, advised me that we could go down by car to get ourselves a little closer to the area of contact, located on the level of the lower mountains and facing the Valley itself. We drove for a stretch down the road and stopped, waiting for a new sign. We knew that, when the vessels materialize themselves or arrive from their missions, the magnetic field of a large area is modified by the dynamic energy they emanate. Thus, it was necessary for us to physically approach these areas gradually and under the command of the vessels. Such command controls the pulsation of the local magnetic field and deeply knows the guests who are going to have these experiences. If they rigorously follow the signals that are transmitted, nothing disharmonious may happen to them; on the contrary, from their inmost self, serene joy will emerge, which will expand the opening of the conscious self, predisposing it to the purification so necessary today.

Before the beginning of the second phase of the physical approach, we remained there unmoving for a few moments. Looking around, we noticed dozens of vessels that made themselves visible, assuring us of their collaboration on all levels. "Everything is under control," confirmed the pleiad. I had never doubted it, but it was also instructive to hear it from an external voice.

On the horizon ahead, the lighting network of the intraterrestrial city of ERKS began to appear before our eyes. We then went a little further and, when close, approximately 200 or 300 meters (600 to 900 feet) from the scene of those events, we stopped. We knew we could not go any further unless we were given authorization. The car was now completely in the dark, the headlights off, leaving us in the middle of the night. The intraterrestrial city lay before our eyes, so that I would later be able to testify to its existence, both through the books I was to write, and the contacts I would have with persons interested in these subjects.

ERKS is called a city, a center or a base, according to the function it is carrying out at the time, and to the level of consciousness of those who contact it. Its existence takes place on several planes, in various dimensions; from a physical point of view, one can say it is subterranean. However, its lights reflect themselves on the surface of mountains that, if seen during the day, present nothing unusual on their peaks. Yet during the night an illumination network shines on it that is not a product of the material electricity that we know, but of the concentration of Ono-Zone energy. That which was presented before my eyes was extremely harmonious and perfectly integrated with the inner and outer aspects of my being.

The expression of ERKS is not fixed; it changes according to the activity that is being developed. There are times when one can see the entrance portal to the city in the form of a series of lights; at other times one can notice the luminosity of the temple, or of the landing bases for the intergalactic space vessels, or even a vast brightness, which may indicate the presence of some being of elevated potency. It is the announced externalization of the Hierarchy, so often promised in the past by the esoteric teachings and by the prophetic texts.

In this opportunity I understood that we – beings incarnated in this end of cycle – can transform ourselves into a field for the fulfillment of the prophecies and a fertile ground where they may materialize themselves. "The highest virtue emerges from the Valley", that ancient yet always new message continued to resound within my interior.

The humanity of the surface of the Earth is being prepared at this time to live in other spheres, among which are the intraterrestrial. Each of these spheres comprises various levels or degrees of consciousness.

Similar to what occurs on the physical, emotional and mental levels of the surface of the Earth, levels where individuals have their experiences according to their own degree of development, so the intraterrestrial and extraterrestrial beings live in different ways, depending on the evolution they have reached. Some are in a corporeal state and follow the material laws of the worlds they belong to; others are in an incorporeal state and submit themselves to other, more subtle laws. Each world has specific ruling laws, according to the stage it finds itself in.

The beings that commanded the vessels that were in front of us, although incorporeal, could physically manifest themselves at will, just as they materialized the vessels they operated and which we could see with our own eyes. Besides the brilliance that they emitted, a brilliance that was a kind of message, at the same time something else was transmitted to us through a kind of inner perception. It was not, however, mental telepathy. It was an omnipresent knowledge, if one could speak in this way. I could experience this state, especially when I "knew" that which was going to happen to me on the following nights. Having remained impassive in the face of that which had been revealed to me, I realized that on all levels of my being there was full acceptance. It is important to make this point clear, because:

> *"That which gives life does not claim any ownership;*
> *It benefits, but does not demand gratitude.*
> *It commands, but does not exercise authority.*
> *This is called the 'mysterious quality'."*

I spent ten nights in the Valley of ERKS: two consecutive nights in the beginning of the month; another three at the end of the same month, and after approximately twenty-five days, when I took a work trip abroad, five more nights. On only two of them the pleiad was not physically with me, because apparently he had other, also important tasks to perform. However, I got to know afterwards that his absence was due, in reality, to my need to prepare myself to remain there in the future without him, for a few hours or for an entire night.

There are some important things to consider with regard to everything that I was allowed to experience. Certain supraphysical realities and inner processes that belong to the sphere of immaterial laws cannot be conceived rationally by the normal individuals from the surface of the Earth. At present, these individuals would demonstrate an intellective coefficient ranging from 8 to 12 out of 100, if we were to compute the totality of their potential.

Take note of the following chart related to the different coefficients of intellectuality:

Current human being from the surface of the Earth		Future human being from the surface	Current evolved intra terrestrial being	Current evolved extraterrestrial being
Normal	Advanced			
$\frac{8}{100}$	$\frac{12}{100}$	$\frac{69}{100}$	$\frac{80}{100}$	$\frac{100}{100}$

An ordinary person would correspond to an 8; a being like Einstein would reach the coefficient 12. However, an intraterrestrial being would achieve the coefficient 80 and an extraterrestrial being can reach up to 100. It will be after the reformation that is being performed on the humanity of the surface, which includes the introduction of new cosmic genes and the presentation of new stimuli to the subtle levels of consciousness, that it will be able to reach the coefficient of 69 over 100.

At this time, it is only when individuals become receptive to the new genetic code and let themselves be transformed by the energies of their supraconsciousness, that their thinking and analytical mind will be able to build a bridge to the abstract mind. This transition is happening with a certain frequency today, and many beings from the surface of the Earth are already integrating themselves into broader levels of reality, that are beyond the physical, emotional and mental levels.

With an intellectual coefficient of 69 over 100, human beings from the surface will be able to live experiences and contacts that up until now were inaccessible to them. To know of this possibility and to use the energy of faith to prepare oneself to get close to supraphyscial realities are requirements for the elevation of consciousness. It is on the basis of this capacity of expansion, available to all, that I narrate my experiences in the Valley of ERKS.

When the genes of incorporeal origin are completely installed in the pituitary gland, and when they assume complete control over the other glands, even during the period of our life on the physical plane, we will be able to participate lucidly in other dimensions of time and space. We will do this by temporarily leaving the body, or by remaining in it, according to the case. In the experience that was reserved for me in the Valley of ERKS, not for a single moment did I lose consciousness on the external level of life. With my human mind, I knew perfectly well what was going on with me – although I had not consciously followed my etheric and emotional bodies when they were taken into the intraterrestrial city. I will try to explain this better in the following pages, though human words are not perfectly adequate to describe supraphysical facts.

In the Valley of ERKS, the area of contacts is active on behalf of the evolution of existence on Earth, but its subjective reality is not physically manifested to the general public. In spite of this, I was given permission to take photos – as photograph ic documentation could be useful in later phases of the work for people who are preparing themselves for similar processes and for new stages in their lives. For this reason I had taken along a camera, a quite ordinary one, which was without any special technical features. In this respect, I learned a few things about it while I was there. I noticed for example, that through the hands of an individual in harmony with superior energies, could pass a certain fluidic current that, in contact with the camera, enables unusual photographs. I also noticed that from the space vessel there could come a creative wave, that adjusts the limitations of the camera and of the photographer, enhancing the capacity of both. Thus, under these conditions, a simple piece of equipment can accomplish work that a powerful telescope handled by a normal astronomer and without the subtle participation of the celestial bodies to perform the task, would not be able to do.

Another particularity that I observed during these contacts was that sometimes I tried to photograph what I saw and the film registered another event. One night, for example, I focused on an image, believing I was photographing the illumination network of the city of ERKS that was visible. However, when the film was developed, we could see subtle bodies of inhabitants of that same city, who apparently had never been in front of my camera.

Not only in the field of photography is there an occult relationship between us and the inner and outer world of beings. The pleiad that accompanied me, communicated with certain celestial bodies that are officially considered to be stars and these bodies, to show me that they were not really stars, responded to his requests. When he said a certain word in the Irdin language, the "star" would disappear from the physical plane; when he emitted another sound in the same language, the "star" reappeared to our concrete vision. According to what he explained to me, the "star" was, in reality a vessel, and for this reason responded in that way to an internal communication. The mantra served for those of us here on the earthly plane as a point of reference. Without the mantra being pronounced, the outer self would find it harder to grasp the mechanism of what was occurring in the inner world, a world that needs no words or phrases in language to express itself and act. In fact, it was the inner transmission that would make the vessel appear or disappear, providing us in this way with the experience we needed. The word pronounced by the pleiad in the Irdin language, a very beautiful one, served therefore for my human aspects to accompany the inner contacts that happened without words between him and the vessel. In order to know this, it is fundamental that we purify ourselves of the spurious emotionalism through the intermediary of which we humans of the surface generally want to contact incorporeal and subtle facts. Reflecting on this can greatly serve to clarify and simplify the way to the inner kingdom of life. After all,

*"The wise ones concern themselves with the inner
And not the outer part of the senses.
They reject the superficial
And prefer to dive into the deep".*

The leap in the dark

Just as to elevate oneself in consciousness when arriving at a certain evolutionary stage, human beings need, in faith, to leap into the void that they find in front of them and entrust their lives to the superior energies, so the Spiritual Beings and Hierarchies, to advance on their paths, have to descend from the elevated plane on which they are polarized, to serve. For this, according to the dictates of this supraphysical law, those who have already reached stages of incorporeal life may return and take up physical bodies on Earth, or on another planet, and act in the three-dimensional world; they may also descend from the planes they are in without materializing themselves and thus work. In order for a real evolution to take place, it is necessary, therefore, that they renounce the state that they have achieved and come in aid of those in most need. The extraterrestrials mentioned here are beings that give of themselves in attunement with this sublime law and, to the extent that humans of the surface of the Earth also adhere to service, they will enter a state of consciousness called brotherhood, a state in which is expressed a love that surpasses all human understanding.

Renunciation, detachment and giving of oneself are the keys to open the doors that lead to the supraphysical worlds. Knowing this, I asked the pleiad about the influence of meditation, of self-control and of a planned rhythm of life in the development of these qualities. He responded to me that such practices are necessary for the phase in which human beings seek for coordination between their bodies, that is, while they work for the harmony of their own being.

However, after following a certain inner way, this harmony will have already been attained, the meditative states will have been established in outer consciousness more firmly, and the vehicles of the personality will no longer need to follow pre-established processes. Of course this does not apply to all individuals, but only to those who have attained a certain degree of harmonization in which a stable contact has been achieved between the higher self and the monad. At this stage, discipline, rhythm and meditation are no longer sought for, because they are always present without requiring any human or mental effort.

The pleiad also told me that the new humanity will no longer have meditative techniques such as are sought after today, or like those developed in the past. The humans with the new genetic code will be ruled by the rhythms of the right-side consciousness, whose centers do not need the work of external meditation, as known up to now.

They will be stimulated to serve the Plan of Evolution which alone will harmonize the inner bodies of an individual. Therefore, schools of the future will be nothing like they are now, based on the development of the human being with the DNA genetic code. In the book MIZ TLI TLAN – *A World that Awakens*, some exercises with signs, symbols and colors were revealed to be used for limited periods of time. They may be utilized today, whether or not the student has developed the stages of the old meditation system.

We already have the knowledge that, for individuals to enter into contact with their own deep levels, and have awareness of the meditative state present there, they would have to be harmonized. But the information given by the pleiade was that, in the future, through the action of the new genetic code GNA, the work we do to practice meditation will no longer be necessary, since human beings will have already reached harmony. These new cosmic genes come from incorporeal worlds and, therefore, do not carry seeds of conflict as did their predecessors.

In transmitting this information I should clarify that I have no intention to devalue any work still being done today in preparation for meditation. One should, however, take into account that the writings that at different times recommended it, were necessarily addressing the needs of human beings with the DNA code. Therefore, they are no longer useful for those who are beginning to be governed by GNA. As we know, all the old discipline was adapted to the development of the masculine polarity of the planet and adjusted itself to the humanity of that time. In other words, the disciplines of yoga and religion dealt directly or indirectly with the known chakras, with the kundalini energy, etc., whereas now, with the development of the feminine planetary polarity, humanity is no longer polarized on the energetic circuit of the chakras, but on the centers that express the right-side consciousness – which is the higher self already incorporated into the external consciousness of the individual. This is why the more lucid instructors of the West (who anticipated modern teaching) never advised present day humanity to focus on the processes related to the chakras.

The energetic circuit of the chakras and kundalini were linked to the activity of the Shamballa center and to the entire Eastern culture; the stimulation of the right-side consciousness, in turn, is linked to the emergence of ERKS and Miz Tli Tlan as planetary centers of great power, that conduct the energy toward the centers of human beings that are awakening today: the right-side mental hemisphere, the right-side cardiac center and the right-side cosmic plexus. The energy of the thinking mind is represented by the head, the energy of feelings, by the heart, and cosmic energy is represented by the plexus situated just below the last rib, on the right-side of the body.

At the present time, students who concentrate on this new distribution of energy in the human being become aware of its reality, just as students of yesterday became aware of the energetic circuit of the chakras.

The pleiad who accompanied me showed me that the energetic system linked to the chakras and to kundalini is connected to the time when human beings exercised their free will – which, according to him, was part of the previous human cosmogony. Also according to the pleiad, we now have the beginning of a higher development of consciousness, a stage in which human beings will transcend free will.

This new stage can already be perceived in certain more awake individuals who can no longer conform themselves to the yoga techniques left by the teachers of the past. In fact, if the great teachers had not been withdrawn from the physical plane, they would have to contradict themselves at each change of planetary cycle, with the advent of new phases of the law. As they began to use the energy of the new cycle, they would lose the credibility of those who were still caught in the web of the intellect. "If all the teachers you know and respect," said the pleiad, "continued to be incarnated and working, they would say different things at each change of cycle." In other words, if Christ were to reincarnate now, he would speak in a different way than Jesus, the Christ, and the Christians themselves might not accept Him. The mind is narrow when conditioned to inert schemes. Because they know little about love-wisdom, humans from the surface of the Earth still do not know how to synthesize the teachings from past cycles and go forward *in the light of the eternal present*. That which the pleiad was trying to express is the need to be open to new expressions of the One Life, which do not annul the old ones, but which develop them, excluding the superfluous elements, often added involuntarily by humanity. "Do not judge that I came to abolish the law or the prophets", said Christ. "I did not come to abolish, but to take them to perfection." (*Matthew.* V, 17).

Taking advantage of the meeting with that being of cosmic consciousness, I asked him what he understood by "pleiad," since this term is used by those genuinely contacted by intergalactic vessels. "Pleiad," he said to me, "is a Hierarchy which, presently, comes from incorporeal worlds and is among humans to carry out the plan of transformation of the planet, a plan that includes the human race and the animal, plant and mineral kingdoms. On the surface of the Earth, we usually use the term pleiad to refer to a constellation. For us, however, a pleiad (in Irdin, we say 'phleich') is anyone who lives in a state of pure energy, without a physical body, and who has decided to take on this dense garment to help in the task of recovering the planet, a task that aims at incorporating it to the conscious cosmic life, with all the attributes that the law of evolution can offer. On the other hand, 'Phleich Yade,' another term in the Irdin language, means inhabitant of all the solar kingdoms, that is, inhabitant of all the suns."

The one who was giving me this information was, himself, a phleich or pleiad, and it was he who was driving the car that was taking us to the area of contacts. His love for truth had made him totally dedicated to evolutionary causes and, at that moment, his work was on Earth. "When did we know each other?" I asked him.

The answer was a little vague. "Our link definitely forged itself when we were Atlanteans." He said no more, because he did not usually talk about reincarnation. According to him, a being can take on a physical body here, without the processes that are normally used for this. In the same way, it can leave the Earth without passing through death, not subject to the law of reincarnation as it is traditionally known, which concerns only those who are under the law of karma of dense matter and, therefore, need to experience birth and death as still happens on Earth. According to the pleiad, there are extraterrestrials that do not have to go through reincarnation and this stage will be accessible to the terrestrials of the surface in a near future.

It might be useful at this point to clarify that we are not affirming that meditation, karma and reincarnation are laws or states that are without effect for most of the humanity, which would be false and ignorant. As we said in the book MIZ TLI TLAN – *A World that Awakens*:

"The astral plane of the three-dimensional world, the plane of the ordinary emotions of humanity of the surface of the Earth, is conditioned by karma, while the cosmic astral plane, which comprises other and different dimensions, can dissolve the karmic situations that humanity from the surface lives in. When one enters this cosmic astral state, free will disappears, and one begins to live a life governed by cosmic laws that are no longer karmic, but that are directly subject to a higher universal order. The evolutionary process is then different; it is no longer a question of living the payments of material karma, but of evolving within a higher, broader understanding and without that which we call suffering."

We ask for attention to this statement, for a part of the humanity of the surface is currently entering this new stage: and some already find themselves liberated from aspects of karma, although they continue to be tied to certain situations due to mere attachment and not to inner necessity. This reflection, accompanied with detachment, can bring much light to crystallized ways of life, transforming them within the law of love.

With respect to these laws the philosopher Paul Brunton, in his posthumous book Perspectives, says: "There are beings not subject to the same laws as those governing humanity's physical existence. They are not normally visible to us. They are gods." (p. 363). Thus, the ones who can see them, are those with cosmic consciousness.

"If Nature keeps her lips inexorably shut to the questions of those who abuse her, she graciously opens them in perfect response to those who ask with a quieted, co-operative and harmonious ego", continues Paul Brunton in the work referred to above (p. 363).

Among the supraphysical laws that will be understood by the humanity of the new Earth we encounter those of supra-nature, which govern the natural laws known today. Through them humanity will be able to control the rain, the winds and the weather and mainly, work with magnetism.

Wide paths are ahead of humanity, and it will see them more clearly when it is no longer centered on the laws of the material world. Under the new genetic code, the GNA, human beings will experience that which in the past was only possible to highly evolved individuals. In reality, the work of these evolved beings was to announce to us, through their testimony, that which will be possible in a subsequent stage for all.

A well-known incarnation process that is uncommon, but which was ruled by non-material laws, was that of the Christ energy in the bodies of Jesus. According to the work of Alice A. Bailey and that of other authors inspired by the Hierarchy, at the moment of Jesus' Baptism in the Jordan River, Christ permeated that adult body, and without the necessity of submitting himself to the well-known law of birth – he incorporated himself to a garment that had already been born and prepared by its previous occupant. This case is not unique and, today, as we know, such opportunities happen with some frequency. They will become quite common in the new Earth, when it is under supraphysical laws, according to what we are going to see next.

Beings that have been freed from the law of death can leave their corporeal garment without it being lost, undergoing involution[15] or disintegrating itself. The body of someone who is free from the law of death can be used by another monad, provided that this body, after it is liberated, is in satisfactory condition for the mission that the new being comes to accomplish. In these cases, the individual disincarnates without going through the normal process of death.

This information came to complete the traditional teachings on death and was totally true for me (who had now undergone another kind of experience) and it resonated within me in the inner as something known. Finally, I was finding myself again, and my

---

[15] Involution refers here to the process of dissolution of the totality of the body and of restitution of its atoms to the planetary ambit.

gratitude was evident. "Gratitude?" asked the pleiad, "gratitude is an indispensable feeling for those who have not yet developed it sufficiently on the human level. However, those who live in a state of union with the essence of Life do not differentiate between the one who gives and the one who receives – gratitude is already so implicit in their being that they do not see any reason to continue externalizing it as a human feeling." This statement prepared me for a state I would experience days later, in an encounter with the vessels in the area of contacts. At this time I realized that my right-side mental center, my right-side heart center and my right-side plexus center responded well to these ideas, giving them a great impulse and completing them. It was as if the pleiad were acting as an instrument for my inner source of knowledge, to awaken new areas of consciousness.

"The goal for bringing you to this area of contacts", he told me about that which I perceived there, "is not to become conditioned to them but to always perceive the need to seek information, to seek the truth. The plan of evolution says that you must go on seeking the truth by yourself, wherever you are – although, as it is evident from this meeting, you are going to be greatly helped and even guided to this." He was looking straight at me when he told me: "Many things are going to happen to you soon."

The dialogue continued while the car got more and more close to the area of contacts. After a curve, we saw a big light appearing in the sky, one that was new to me. "And that one?" I asked. It was a space vessel from the largest active intraterrestrial center: Miz Tli Tlan, situated in the subtle counterpart of the Peruvian Andes. It appeared looking like a star and gradually started radiating a light of violet color, forming a gigantic halo. When the crown of light became quite visible, it was confirmed that it was not a star. During the following nights of this cycle of contacts, this vessel was always present. It certainly had deep meaning for us and to our present work on Earth.

When observing the sky, one can have a "sui generis" view of it, facilitated by the presence of special elements among those already known. Each space vessel, for example, has the ability to control what an individual can or cannot see, so that an ordinary astronomer, without elements of intuitive perception, may even document a "sky" that, in reality, does not exist. This space vessel I have just mentioned is considered to be an important star. However, when in contact with us, it moved about and openly demonstrated to us what we have just related. A person with a rational mind would be perplexed in the face of what we were seeing: for to demonstrate to us their ability to control laws that we do not know on the physical plane, this space vessel covered itself with clouds that it created in order to not to be seen. Once we had grasped this message, it returned to behaving like a star, an element known to terrestrial astronomy. We already knew that there are celestial bodies considered to be planets that in reality are not, and others, considered to be satellites, that are space vessels controlled by systems that, are often, many light-years away. The pleiad affirmed as well, that some discoveries are yet to be made by humanity with respect to the Sun (or suns), because according to him that which we call Sun is, in fact, three stars and not one, the Moon, and planets important for life on Earth.

There are space vessels that function for millions of years and that, depending on their cosmic task, appear to us to be stable in the sky. Their ability to emit light or to manipulate it, which I learned about in part during the contact I had in the Valley of ERKS, opened me to new concepts that displaced many of the beliefs that had been transmitted to me by current astronomy. And what to say about real stars that no longer exist, and that we consider to be active, due to the fact that their light is still on its way to the Earth, covering the great distance that separates them? Considering these stars that no longer exist physically, as well as the intergalactic vessels we referred to, that function in long-term missions (which leads them be considered planets or stars), it seems to us that the map of the sky should always be reformulated by intuitive and clairvoyant individuals (in the inner sense of the word and not just the psychic sense). This planet has other pleiades besides the instructor who accompanied me during the experience in the Valley of ERKS. They are ready to collaborate with us in updating our knowledge about the sky, but they have not yet been heard by the scientists from the surface of the Earth.

During the nights of work in the area of contacts, we saw clouds moving against the wind, or clouds that remained still and static, in places of great turbulence with winds so strong they almost brought our camera tripod to the ground. "Clouds follow intelligent orders and not always the wind," said the pleiad in the face of the evidence that was before us. And he added: "The same happens with water, which does not follow only the force of gravity." According to him, the water in a valley can flow up a mountain, provided that it is given an intelligent order that comes from supraphysical levels. This "command" that water receives and which it follows is based on laws of antimatter and not on the laws we know. When a solid body is transported, even if at least partially, to a supraphysical dimension, all of it is passed under the influence of laws from that higher plane, therefore behaving differently or "abnormally" if seen from a conventional terrestrial viewpoint.

In the area of contact, in addition to the Miz Tli Tlan vessel, there were hundreds of others. Not only there, but also other areas of the planet have many of them. The same is true in the subsoil of the Moon. These vessels, as was explained in the book MIZ TLI TLAN – *A World that Awakens*, are prepared for different operations in the Earth's orbit. They will go into action if there is another atomic war, or a little before a change in inclination of the Earth's magnetic axis.

The pleiad, the person with whom I was having a conversation and who was my guide, knew a great deal about this process, about which we had already developed some topics in previous works, such as, for example, ERKS – *Inner World*. Such facts indicate an opportunity for transformation. The law of purification is, in fact, a reward for those who have reached the limit point to change planes, to change the level of consciousness. Through this law, one enters a higher round of the spiral of evolution and begins to live under broader laws, disengaged from the suffering of present times.

Independently from what is its externalization on the physical and psychic planes, the purifying law is lived by humanity of the surface in four stages:

> 1. inner spiritual purification, which human beings can achieve, often unconsciously, throughout their incarnations;
>
> 2. knowledge of cosmic laws, which are transmitted to them as a consequence of the preceding stage;
>
> 3. liberation from death, as has been illustrated here;
>
> 4. liberation from physical birth, taking into consideration that which occurs on the surface of the Earth.

In the following chapters, I will share my conscious experiences of these four stages of the law of purification. While I clearly know that certain supraconscious facts were the most significant ones, for the time being my mind did not have access to them. We can see that this book has limits determined by a plane that is above the one who writes about it at the present moment.

Part Two

The Nights of ERKS

*"If the spirits lost their transcendence,
they would probably disappear."*

The first night

When an individual reached the center of the Great Pyramid, they were asked why they had come there and why the normal paths, followed by almost everyone, were not good enough for them. If they hesitated, nothin g would happen within them; if they answered promptly that the normal paths no longer interested them, then the process known by liberated beings would begin.

If the candidates answered that they sought nothing besides the inner path that led to cosmic union, a second test was given to them: they, as candidates to the understanding of the universal laws, were invited to return to the agitation and attractions of the crowds, to the entertainment, to material comfort, so that they might forget this longing for the path of ascent. Given such options, the person could accept the invitation, or answer that it would be impossible for them to return.

Those who took the second option were told that the path they had chosen would take them to extreme limits, and not all who took it could remain sane. It was also explained that there was still time to give up these trials. In most cases, however, the candidates seeking liberation from the yoke of material laws reaffirmed their intentions, because at a certain point, there was no other path for them to follow. They would, then, become aware of the fact that they would lose all formal ties with "the world," even if they went on living in it formally. If knowing this, they confirmed their initial intentions, they would hear a sentence that could be thus expressed, "Now you cannot go back. You are a blessed one."

There has always been this secret dialogue that individuals maintained with the Guides who worked with them on the inner levels of life, preparing them for decisive steps in the evolutionary ascent. Within this sacred scheme, events took place in the caverns or in the temples of the physical plane and, at the same time, in the inner and subjective caves of beings, who in this way left their condition of submission to material laws to enter the knowledge of the immaterial ones.

In the Valley of ERKS, we did not have this dialogue, although ERKS is the center that, in this epoch, has the task of leading human beings more directly to higher states of consciousness. In the Valley of ERKS, this dialogue was given as implied. There was total knowledge of that which was happening inwardly and outwardly and, even if the physical brain or the human personality did not notice anything, the state of calm would never be interrupted. In the Valley of ERKS, when one is accepted, their decision is already known, and one knows that there is no return, even if the person is tempted to; their Guides not only know the person deeply, but they also do not believe it necessary to ask them questions. In this sense, there are no formalities or tests. Times have changed, although mysteries always exist.

On the way to the Valley, while still in the car, a deep calm invade d my being. It was not only calm; something else took hold of me forever and led me I did not know where to. I let myself be led from that moment on, without offering resistance. The pleiad was driving the car, and this, too, had a symbolic meaning: moments later, he would be the external guide of the ceremony that was to realize itself.

"I feel I have been emptied of something, but I do not know of what. Anyway, I feel very well," I told him. The pleiad smiled lovingly, because he knew this subject very well. "Your emotional and etheric bodies are being taken to ERKS. They will continue to be linked to you by only a thread. Do you notice this?" he asked me. "Clearly," I responded. Then I remained in silence and nothing more was said until we reached the top of the mountain.

I had finished writing a book about ERKS,[16] and this center was for me more than a cause for subjective study. I knew that, physically, it was some miles below ground but, in other dimensions, one encountered it everywhere, as a state of consciousness. Therefore, the fact that my bodies were taken there, as the pleiad said, with great tranquility, also was for me, natural. In a certain sense, I felt myself internally there, although my human and brain consciousnesses remained lucid about what was happening on the physical plane of my life at that moment and, not for even an instant, did I feel myself to be in a trance or alienated from the outer world.

As the car continued up the mountain, I experienced the sensation of not being only on this Earth. I am using the word sensation here, but this is not exactly what was present in me. Everything that I

---

[16] ERKS-*The Inner World*.

"felt" in those moments was felt in a form different from that which I had always felt. I was starting to experience *some* feeling inside of me: but it was no longer me who felt.

There, at the very top, we waited for the great vessel to give the signal that we could approach. A great love united me to everything and, in a special way, to the energy coming from the space vessel, a balm that will never leave me. Looking at the horizon, to the end of the Valley, we saw the space vessel-light calling us.

I had no intention to personalize any facts, yet certain names were becoming known to my consciousness at that moment. They were cosmic names in the Irdin language which, when pronounced by the pleiad, kept the general vibration high within a radius of many miles. All of them were old acquaintances, but still the names that were presented kept displacing schemes from my human mind, schemes that still lasted. Each scheme that fell was one more liberation for me, it was one area of my being undergoing clarification, it was a deep, subjective breathing.

At that moment, with the space vessel calling us, even if we wanted, it would be impossible to have emotions. All reminiscence, that by chance emerged from the subconscious, was dissolved. There, nothing else existed but the present instant.

I was empty of emotions and of purely physical vitality. I was experiencing another physical state, and the feeling that emerged was far gentler than those I had known until then. "We don't expect you to behave in prescribed ways," the pleiad told me. "Be at ease, take photos if you want to." Although this may seem strange, everything I will describe next, happened while I was taking photographs. The formality of the ancient mystical rituals was coming apart before my eyes and my senses.

In fact, all this had been prepared for centuries but my consciousness had taken little notice of it. At each incarnation a new physical brain is formed, and the human memory of a certain life does not include what happened in the previous ones. Even the so-called "body" of the soul, the causal body that stores past events, keeps them veiled in the memory until a real need to bring them to the surface arises.

Thus, it was not at all important that I have any formal attitude during these solemn moments (or, more importantly, in this earthly incarnation); and, in order for me to not have doubts that the greatest value lay in that which had been prepared within me throughout the centuries, the pleiad kept repeating, "Take photos, be at ease."

Intuition was telling me that in the Valley of ERKS there was the synthesis of such a vast past that no earthly chronology could recompose it. My earthly lives in Lemuria, in Atlantis and, finally, the most recent ones – including that which was happening there, in the Valley – were all known to the archives of ERKS. The reality of this event was recognized without giving importance to facts. Whenever some fact revived itself, it was only to help loosen inner ties. It was synthesis that we were really looking for, and this is what prevailed. A synthesis that says always, "Forward!" And forward one goes.

As we descended the hillside, reaching an area that was a lot closer to the space vessels that were maneuvering, the pleiad, between phrases in Irdin that he directed to the vessels, helped me adjust the camera tripod, because, being a beginner in this subject, I could not manage to make it work on my own. As we placed the camera in a new position, he asked me, "Do you feel well?" "I've never felt so well," I replied. My emotional body and my etheric body kept connected to my physical body by only a thread because they had been taken to ERKS, the center whose lights were reflected high up on the mountain. I knew

I would have no awareness of what was happening to them, and this was so for reasons that I would never be able to fully understand. However, two of these reasons were clear to me: the first one was that I had to go through the trial of letting my bodies leave, guided by other energies, with nothing to fear; the other was that I should keep my consciousness totally linked to the physical body, so that later I would be able to share these events in a concrete manner, accessible to the others. That which I am narrating will happen to many individuals in the new phase of the Earth. It is no longer a rare fact, circumscribed to a secret room of a pyramid, as it used to be.

A great need for solitude descended upon me, as a consequence of the work that was being done in ERKS on my subtle bodies. I withdrew, while I took photos and heard the chants of the pleiad in the dark of night. There were times when we left the car headlights on, but most of the time they were kept off. I felt a deep withdrawal, not only the need for it. "After you get back your emotional body, more worked on, you will be able to take on tasks that were impossible before. Are you prepared for this?" the pleiad asked me.

With this question he was not presenting me one of those classical tests that were given to the candidates to knowledge of immaterial laws: tests on overcoming fear, on the presence of faith, on the control of nerves. All these had already been acquired. The tasks referred to were with reference to works to be done here on planet Earth. I had already accepted them without even knowing what they were. "Tonight you are being prepared for what is going to happen tomorrow. Soon your bodies will return, but do not focus your attention on these facts. Continue taking photos," he said to me.

I could notice the law of purification acting inside of me and outside of me. What took place externally and internally conveyed this. I experienced an inner calm that I could never have achieved on my own, and the night was filled with love, with will and with an intelligent activity visibly written in the skies. The external was like the internal: full of peace.

About thirty-three space vessels moved themselves in a perfect rhythm. Some smaller vessels were released from inside some of them. Some were on specific maneuvers, but others were there for us. They rejoiced in the spiritual opportunity we were being given. I realized this by means of an inner sensitivity, for the movements they made were always silent. All that joy was internalized, and, thus, participating in it, I could realize how much those beings of cosmic consciousness value the fact that someone is beginning on the path of return to the kingdom that belongs to all. Great parties take place in the heavens every time a being returns to the house of the *Father*.

Yes, a great party was going on there, within and outside of us. The pleiad also rejoiced. I realized then that my life was becoming more conscious and I would no longer be the same. "At last!" he said in a raised voice – and I knew what this meant.

I always knew that I had never been alone during my efforts; now, however, I could see with my physical eyes the beings who had always accompanied me and who were present there, creating a night like this one and merging with me, so that my gratitude and joy were internalized without limits in manifesting love and power.

A vessel accompanied us during the entire trip back to the hotel where we were spending the night, and I could see it through the car window. To me that meant something that would never end. To know that I would eternally be aware of being accompanied, followed, helped, so that I could do something for my fellow beings or for beings from other kingdoms was a reality that was imprinting itself deeply in my being, something that the bodies of my personality would never forget.

Everything that had formerly been mental, intellectual and human processes transformed themselves from that night on, into a reality on another level. All the experiences lived previously, that had been based on faith, modified themselves until they, lovingly, disappeared – and a new state installed itself in my being.

While driving, a little before we arrived at the hotel, the pleiad told me, "In the new cosmogony we will not be linked to free will; therefore, we should no longer pay attention to the chakras, but instead be established on three levels: head (symbol of the thinking human), heart (symbol of the new astral condition), and cosmic plexus (situated a little below the last rib on the right-side of the body), and symbol of contact with cosmic energies." However, he was not referring only to the physical body. These points were reflections of that which should happen in the individual's consciousness. It meant that we should transcend free will to embrace internally and externally a deeper will. I could understand everything with tranquility. If we were in the time of the pyramids, my guide would have indicated a sarcophagus for me to lie down in. Now, however, inside that car, it was enough to be totally alert to what the pleiad said between the lines and connected to what occurred within me.

It was past midnight when we arrived at the hotel. I went straight to my room, avoiding any abrupt movement that could disturb the state of inner quietude that I found myself in. The hotel was silent, and at that time of year there were very few guests. As I prepared to sleep I could not wonder about what had happened, because as soon as I lay down my physical body fell into deep sleep. For years I have been sleeping a maximum of four hours a night, and so it was on that night. However, when I woke up from the physical sleep, I had the impression of having slept for an eternity.

The pleiad explained to me that it was during deep sleep that we can be the most transformed. It was clear to me that the work had not been interrupted when we physically left the Valley of ERKS. It would always happen, it would never end. It is real on all levels, and I consciously knew of its action.

Ever since these facts happened, I feel that I am always helped invisibly. I began to permanently live the experience that we are never left on our own when we renounce human free will. Then I perceived that I should talk about all this, as I am doing now, so that we will no longer hesitate when facing the evolutionary opportunities that life brings us. We must understand that real freedom lies in not doing what we want, but in seeking to transcend the childish stage of satisfying desires. Once we overcome this stage, the energy of the being begins to follow a deeper, and more true will and, when we the least expect it, we enter a state that words cannot describe. From then on, explanations are unnecessary.

The night of the baptism

If the experiences that I went through had occurred at the time of the pyramids and of the ancient temples, the space vessels I saw before me would have been a retinue o f priests and hierophants; the pleiad would have been one of those solemn characters, a symbol of love, of service and of wisdom, guiding me through the ceremony. In Antiquity, a sanctuary was known by few; nowadays, in the Valley of ERKS, it is a cosmic campanile open for all to see, although not always perceived in its inner and subjective aspect.

The walls of the ancient temples and of the pyramids were ornamented with works that recounted for the candidates the history that they should know, in this way helping them enter new states of consciousness. In the Valley of ERKS, such works are part of the mountains that, when looked at, evoke in the observer inner meanings. One can see there forms created when the region was the bottom of the ocean, forms that, for millions of years, have resisted transformation. Some present the feminine aspect of the human being; others remind us of the opposite aspect, the masculine. "Uniting these two aspects, harmonizing them, one goes up an important step of the evolutionary scale" – those millenary stones in the Valley of ERKS seemed to say to me.

Those symbols, sculptured in a natural way in the rocks, said as well, as did the ancients, that "the human being never dies". Yes, the death human beings fear, is an appearance. To have been temporarily freed from the emotional and etheric bodies, to experience that state the pleiad called the spiritual, brought me the impression of being purified. I knew that the astral and etheric bodies would have to completely return after a period, but I did not have in myself any anxiety in relation to it. After a few days I unexpectedly realized that they were again present, but that I found myself transformed.

At a certain moment, the pleiad told me that in the times of Lemuria I had a very positive incarnation interrupted, but that now I was healed of the residues of that experience. Thus, I was going to receive a new task.

I asked nothing about this task, because I knew everything happens in its own time. I had renounced being given any kind of explanation, no matter how essential it might seem to be. In this state of freedom and surrender, came to me unexpectedly a name that signified, in our words *I am the Kingdom*. "You are hearing this name from the point of view of a certain plane of consciousness. As, however, you change planes through service, you will hear different names. The names do not designate individuals, but tasks, works, missions." That was for me very clear and the name I heard was very familiar. It had nothing to do with my present name, or with those I had during all my lives on this Earth or in other worlds. But that was my unpronounceable name.

I had always suspected that the names used by us on Earth meant almost nothing. No matter how many mental and esoteric interpretations we give to them, they are really worth very little. Even the most sacred ones, those most used in the ancient writings are relative – that is, above them there is always a greater name. How far can we go, humanly designating that which has no limitations? What need is there to name the un-nameable, to limit the limitless?

Although they correspond only to a certain level of consciousness and not to others, elevated words can help us in our moments of silence. While certain phrases came before my memory (certainly not by chance) and, having before me that which was going on in the Valley of ERKS, I deeply longed for quietness.

This second night was very silent also, on the physical plane. The pleiad almost never spoke, except at certain moments, to help me understand facts that for me were unheard of. I knew that, in no former incarnation, in no other world, in no other planet, had I ever passed through anything similar. In other times, they would have said in my ear, "You have learned the lesson. Keep it forever." But there, at that moment, nothing was said to me. The vessels continued their movement, which seemed to constitute an immense meditation.

The great vessel of the High Command for the Rescue Operation; the vessel of the High Command for all the area of ERKS; the vessel that represented the creative source for the mutation planned for the Earth, a mutation that turned itself irreversible from the date we have already mentioned; the vessel commanded by the being who works in the recovery of those who truly feel the call to inner change and who respond to this call (this being, Ashtar Asghran, was sending me a special ray of love and, at a certain moment, I felt our deep union); the vessel that represented the link between this current terrestrial civilization and the major Hierarchies of ERKS; the vessel of the harmony of the universe, feminine creative source of the new human race of the surface of the Earth, as the pleiad would call it in his devotional invocations; the vessel that contained energies from distinct universes, bringing thus a ray of union to all the Hierarchies; the vessel that represented a planet far from Earth (about 500 light-years), and that had recently been incorporated into the Intergalactic Council (this vessel, of a special radiance, acts as Informational Hierarchy for its own planet); finally, the vessel representing all the intraterrestrial energies of our world.

Also there was a Council made of elders, a Council that controls the life and the organization of the city of ERKS, situated miles below the land that on the surface appears as the Valley.

The night was silent. In ninety minutes by the earthly clock an eternity passed-itself. Lights appeared behind the mountains, on the physical plane. Beings coming from other intraterrestrial centers (some of these centers were bigger than ERKS) made themselves visible in this way. In these cases, I did not see vessels, but only immense lights. Suddenly, a larger light drew itself near, crossing the Valley. It seemed to come to meet us. It was still far when the pleiad announced: "This one represents your monad. It is the Energy that comes to take over you." It was Ashtar Asghran, instructor of the monads.

The fact happened without greater obstacles, and without my vitally noticing it. From then on, I was someone else, only this. That light which represented, on the physical plane, my Formation Guide – of which is impossible to explain, as it is also impossible to transmit in words what this "take over you" is. It has nothing to do with any earthly idea. I realized that "I was formed," that "I am formed," that "I will always be formed" and that his formation will never end. This was my Guide.

On that silent night, I noticed inwardly, that I would live the following nights without bringing my camera with me. "Yes," said the pleiad, "leave it aside for a while." The tripod had then been put in the car, and all the equipment packed up, when the order came to me, "Look at the valley. Do you see the energy?" Yes, I could see it. From one end of the valley to the other hovered something subtle in the atmosphere, something that looked like mist, but it was not – these beings had formed it. The light that was my Guide had become completely internalized. The silence was deep, perceptible. "Go," said the pleiad almost in a hush, "they are calling, walk across the valley. Go through that energy."

I started to walk. The rocks on the narrow road were not an obstacle. There was a slope that my physical eyes could not perceive very well. It was then that an event took place suddenly: a full moon, brighter than I had ever seen, appeared from behind a hill and lit up the way to a point that I could even see my shadow projected on the ground. The bright moonlight was not just light. The whole right-side of my body was touched by these rays. I found a part of myself in ERKS – the emotional and etheric bodies – the biggest part of them for sure, and the symbol of that which occurred there was represented by the light of the Moon that covered the right-side of my body.

This process can be studied by those who aspire to free themselves from the terrestrial material laws. For this I will describe it within the limits permitted by words. At this time, the work of the beings who visit the Earth takes place on three levels:

- on the physical, where a preparation of individuals for the change of genes and the implantation of new micro-organs in each organ of the present body takes place;

- on the spiritual, where a purification that reaches all the supraphysical planes that need it takes place;

- on the cosmic level, the consciousness of the being amplifies itself so that it can contact universal knowledge.

Such opportunity is available to all and, when the individual recognizes it as the only goal in their life, the energies respond and all that is necessary organizes itself. Whether one is aware of this or not, the inner self (the cosmic essence here on earth that we call monad or spirit places the person before new laws. This happens this way because the individual has awakened to the only purpose for their existence.

While walking, I realized that the car driven by the pleiad was following me with the headlights off. He was the symbol, on the physical plane, of the inner Guide that my human consciousness had just recognized. This second night, I had walked enough and it was time to return to the hotel. Resounding within my soul, in my mind, and in all my being, was something similar to "There is an incorporeal state that does not procreate". But only during the following visits to the Valley of ERKS would I understand what this meant. In that moment it was only necessary for me to perceive that the distance between the Earth and the incorporeal worlds exists only in the mental substance; in reality, these worlds are very close, and we can contact them if we open ourselves to them.

This is what went on with my being that night, which I have called the night of Baptism: the spiritual energy of the Great Fraternity, represented by the space vessels, served as a means so that the cosmic energy could be introduced to my human levels. Among those celestial intermediaries (I prefer to call them this way there was a Hierophant (Ashtar Asghran who, symbolically, at that moment, instructed my incarnated monad and two other intermediators who constituted the electric positive and negative polarities of the energy.

During those instants, my higher self was a negative polarity in respect to my monad and, at the same time, a positive polarity in respect to my personality. This double role it fulfilled with ease, without my feeling any division. The balance was perfect, at least from the point of view of the conscious self.

While the celestial intermediators enabled the introduction of cosmic rays into all of my being, my higher self enabled the introduction of cosmic life into my human part. The city of ERKS worked together with my higher self. The pleiad, who had accompanied me (since Atlantis, in perfect union, as he said declared he was "ERKS doorkeeper" and this designation left me speechless, because I started to feel that, from then on, I would also be useful to other beings, that were inwardly linked to me by bonds of eternal love.

From that night on was put in motion an energetic process that could never be interrupted. My being had entered a cosmic current from which there was no more possibility of return. It was for this reason that the pleiad radiated such internal joy as he said, "At last!"

These perceptions were not imaginative creations but were a synthesis of what had happened to me up to then, so that my consciousness could prepare itself for an event that was forseen for three weeks later.

Three weeks later

After these first facts, I returned to the capital of the country, where an extensive public work waited for me. Arriving there, my friends remarked that I had changed a lot. To some I explained that I had gone through a kind of healing, and that mainly my emotional body had been worked on inwardly by positive and conscious energies that were aware of my evolution.

I felt a new vibration circulating in me and, from then on, even if I tried, I could no longer be emotional as before. A deep feeling of internal union, of openness, of gratitude and of peace never left me. Thus in this way, I could spend three weeks as if time and space had become rarefied, without weight, without gravity, without any kind of attachment. At the end of each public conference that I made, would come to me the confirmation of a great internal unity with everything and everyone, and the magnetic wave that flowed through me and through what I said, was different from the previous one. People noticed this and openly referred themselves to this transformation. However, none of this was emphasized nor dramatized; life proceeded normally, although many knew that I had been in contact with the Valley of ERKS.

The facts that took place in the "Night of Baptism" prepared my higher self to establish an effective contact between my physical consciousness and the astral-emotional. From that moment and after, all emotional activity could be controlled with intelligence. The mind, in its turn, could expand its abilities, establishing a link between its thinking area and its abstract area -- this latter is called "over-mind" in some classical books of spiritual philosophy.

In the soul, or the higher self, were shining brilliant expansions of light from the supramental levels.

In the outer life, service was to be expanded, and this was the central fact that most affected me, according to my temperament at that time.

For the persons who were together with me during those days, was a period of training in observation of the presence of subjective facts manifested in the physical plane itself. I, on the other hand, was going through trials of a kind, to adapt me completely to states of feeling and ways of seeing completely unknown. New energies turned themselves more intense in my consciousness, and the synthesis of my Lemurian past was brought to my human knowledge. I found in it many liberating keys for the present time. Seeing, during these studies, how empty the previous psychological analyses had been.

That which happened on the following nights is not fit to be narrated in a chronological way. The description of time, of the rhythm of the days, of the states of consciousness, followed an internal movement and not a mental sequence. It would be important, now, that the reader have in mind some stages of the law of purification, the protagonist of the entire process that I went through. It was with this law in mind, that I told the pleiad during one of our car trips to the Valley of ERKS, "I can't explain how, but I *know* I am going to live a great transformation." "Yes," he affirmed promptly, "it won't be long until it happens."

We were driving along the dirt road while a space vessel accompanied us in the sky, to my right. I looked at it, greeted it, and said to the pleiad, "If it has to happen, I am ready." "Yes, it is going to happen," he repeated, and began chanting mantras, while driving.

Arriving at the top of the mountain, getting out of the car, I put on a robe that I had been given by the pleiad to be worn there and during any other vigil I made. Everything was in order on the physical plane. On the internal planes, I felt a detachment that I had never before experienced. Normally, we accustom ourselves to thinking that, when the time comes for the transmutation[17], one has great difficulty in letting go of things from this Earth. For me, this did not occur. While observing with clarity that my inner being would be living the experience of transmigration to other planes, to other worlds beyond this solar system, no part of me offered resistance. I was at ease, relaxed, without any sign of discomfort of any kind.

And thus it happened: the interior being departed without the human consciousness even noticing it. I stood there, sometimes talking to the pleiad, other times listening to what he said or chanted. I observed the vessels that were helping this process of mine, but I never thought about myself, about what might happen, or what might already be happening to me. The security and the peace that I felt were total.

---

[17] See chapter about the Law of Transmutation in the Appendix of this book.

Suddenly I realized that a great distance separated my human consciousness from that one that had always inhabited my body, or the bodies that my ego knew. Yes, there was a physical distance of light-years between the individual who observed and that one who, without being perceived, had departed on a great journey. I remained very still inwardly for a moment; however without even feeling that I was left on my own.

The pleiad revealed then that the inner being that had just transmigrated had fulfilled its tasks here on Earth and was, therefore, liberated. As he said the word "liberated," I felt a great jubilation. I was participating in the joy of that incorporeal state where that one who had inhabited these bodies found itself. Thus, I realized that physical distances count for little.

I did not know to where the inner being that I had known as the main part of myself during my whole life had gone; yet I did not feel separation. "The one in you now has a more expanded consciousness. This helps your conscious human side to see more broadly". Yes, there was no merit in my material aspect, not in my personality—this was evident to me; everything was due to supraphysical levels, mine and of those cosmic beings who were giving signs of their presence around there.

"Everything is completely under control," said the pleiad. "Do you feel any discomfort?" "None," I responded, "there is a small spot on the right side of my neck that seems a little sore, nothing else." The pleiad repeated, "Everything is well controlled" – and he looked at the vessels.

Thus happened the transmigration of the inner being that had inhabited this physical-emotional-mental garment for a certain period, and the transmutation of the inner being that will inhabit it until a certain task is completed. During the transmutation, the physical body and the conscious self felt nothing, maintaining themselves always lucid. When, after what had occurred, I concentrated my human mind in a more intense way in the center of my being, I noticed there was another energy there. "You are going to notice it more clearly as days go by," said the pleiad, smiling. "Little by little, you will know it better."

However, it was as if I already knew it very well. It was as though I had known it from before. Then I saw that mystery is always present. So deep was our union that I almost forgot my inner self had left to have another experience. Aware of this, I felt only gratitude growing within. But it was gratitude that came not only from within me – it also came from "far away", from many light-years away.

❖ ❖ ❖

Between the inner being that had gone, the inner being that was here and the conscious being (or personality, there was no separation. Even though I knew, inside and outside of me, that the one who had left was now living another life – free – my human consciousness was ready to continue its earthly cycle and to take on the tasks that the new being was clearly bringing with him.

With time, said the pleiad, who accompanied all that process, I would get to know the new being better. "This new being" – he pointed to me – "had not descended into the corporeal state for about two thousand years. He had spent a long time on planets of incorporeal life." I noticed that a complete harmony was coming over me. There were no difficulties.

I watched the vessels going around us and deeply felt the help I had received. My physical eyes saw that night sky, all spotted with stars and vessels, many light-years away… What are distances? What do they mean? All was well, and peace reigned within and outside of my being.

That which has always been called "the freeing of the spirit" left no dramatic marks on me. The physical body and the other levels of the personality maintained themselves calm while the inner being moved away, and they did not show the least sign of disharmony with the arrival of the new being. Life was always present, and the awareness of being alive in each moment did not remove itself. I realized then, in terms of help, what the presence of laboratory-vessels and of beings that had transcended the law of birth and death represented.

I remembered to myself that, in past times, all this would pass mixed with states of trance, or with trials considered to be suffocating to the human garment. At that moment I looked at the sky and saw as many vessels as there were beads on the necklace that the pleiad had given me on one of the previous nights. Everything was perfectly interconnected and absolutely nothing happened by chance there.

"The transmutation was easy because there was correct preparation," said the pleiad, continuing with his task of teaching me.

There are beings that go to the supraphysical world without suffering attachments and without anxiety; others come to the physical world equally free of problems and pains. "They are transmuted," said the pleiad. "There are neither birth pains, nor the usual death-rattle of letting go. With the transmutation process, there is no death or birth." Out of this Earth, there are worlds and states of consciousness in which procreation, as we know it, is not necessary; birth constitutes itself simply as a materialization coming from the spiritual individual's own subtle bodies. Neither is there "death" or "disincarnation", in such cases. The beings transmute, change planes, just as happened to the inner being that used to be in this body that is writing now.

"Humanity can be liberated from the law of birth and of death," reaffirmed the pleiad.

Although everything was presented in such a simple way, I knew there were night prayers around me. It was a question of prayers of light, not petitions for requests: they were radiations from those who, in the space vessels, were in permanent vigil. The union I felt with them cannot be expressed in words.

I had always known that death was no more than an appearance, but now I understood also the uselessness of this appearance. Right there was a garment ready to act, think and feel, in which transmutation had taken place imperceptibly. Yes, death is a creation of humans who still are subject to the most dense material laws.

The aim of the rituals in ancient temples was to show to the students that "death does not exist". Such teaching was adjusted in a practical way to give to them an experience of everything that a dying person experiences, and to then guide them to the other side of the veil of existence. Coffins or sarcophagi were used for this. The mountains of the Valley of ERKS were my sacred sarcophagus (that had nothing mournful about it and the celestial dome, showing on the horizon the lights of the city of ERKS, was the other side of the veil. The experience constituted itself in a flash of non-material light and of a human garment as a tranquil and unshakable observer.

Initiates say that ancient high priests had the power to keep the students' mind awake while their bodies remained in a trance; thus, they could go through the supraphysical or supra-terrestrial experience and recall it when returning to their normal state. In past times, hypnotism was almost always used for this purpose. Today one can perceive the interpenetration of all the worlds without leaving the conscious state and without experiencing any symptom of trance or unconsciousness.

These processes in the past served to demonstrate the reality that the inner being is immortal. Today, the knowledge of immortality, as idea, is partly incorporated into human beings of the surface of the Earth and, because of this, the ceremonies carried out by the vessels during their contact with us can be very simple.

The body of my monad can live on incorporeal levels and it is only my garment that sees it as a body. The monad can be completely free when it finishes its mission on Earth; but, when it is finished, I know that compassion will bring it to use this freedom to descend to a lower plane another time to serve the others.

In ancient times, the initiate had to plead and submit him or herself to anguishing tests, because the formation took place on concrete levels. In my experience, pleadings were not necessary and the tests, I did not know them. I know that the cosmic being that we all are, sees when things should happen to us, if they need to happen.

The times change. Now it is from the subtle planes of consciousness that the priests of the cosmos prepare the candidates. On supraphysical levels they train them for the use of force, and, on the supramental levels, for the use of the will. Regarding the physical body it is prepared through the incorporation of the new genetic code and the implantation of new micro-organs, according to the new planetary laws.

That which was formerly called the "saving grace offered by the gods" is today permanent grace, that never abandons us, even when we do not see the vessels or the Hierarchies present in them. Ashtar Asghran, in front of me as light, gave me the experience of normality.

The pliead would occasionally, while chanting mantras in Irdin during the ceremony, put his hand on my head; but he would do it in an imperceptible way and without the slightest dramatization. On those nights in the Valley of ERKS, before going, I usually passed the day with only fruit and, during the day, sometimes only on liquids (following the pleiad's suggestion, but returning to our place after midnight, we would have a snack together and share brief comments, reconstructing parts of the ceremony. Yes, the pleiad was an old acquaintance, who knew very well how to perform the work of a sacerdote. As we know, a true sacerdote is not a mere ritualist, but is a being who knows the higher law and lives by it. A true sacerdote is not a member of any caste, but is a member of a level of consciousness. There are many members of the sacerdotal caste on Earth, but few are genuine sacerdotes. To be a sacerdotal, in the sense of being the law, it is not necessary to belong to earthly castes.

While the pleiad officiated at the ceremony, the Highest Priest shone before us. His light will never be forgotten.

Phases of purification

The process of purification goes through various phases in the inner, on the spiritual path. Initially, it takes place on the human level, across various lives; but it is not this purely human experience we are going to deal with here, but the phases that follow. And it is only from the moment when human beings change their own thinking state, that they transcend the first phase of this process, surpassing involvement with forces of earthly matter and with their own human and psychological aspects.

While remaining polarized in the ordinary mind, they live mere struggles and alternate between different states of disharmony; but changing the form of thinking, decentralizing itself from their ego, and becoming aware of real and broader needs, of groups or of humanity, finally they enter another energetic vibration. It is at this point that they become truly useful to the Plan of Evolution, and not before when they find themselves still involved in personal and material questions.

In the first phase, purification includes suffering, so much that the common ideas with respect to this are linked to concepts of loss, pain, destitution and punishment. However, this first phase of purification, overcoming itself, goes on to a different way of understanding.

Purification, for those who have changed their own thinking state, speaks of freedom from all kinds of ties with the Earth and with the dense material vibration. For this to happen, there is the action of the higher energy of the monad, which already controls the higher self and incarnates according to precise phases to be lived. In the stages of development of the human personality, the order is to identify oneself with matter; and next is the beginning of awareness of the higher self, which leads to a relative involvement, through means of services rendered to matter. However, in the stages of monadic contact, the energy changes and deals with liberating itself, to participate in more broad services.

I have the awareness of having gone through this liberating process, and that the work carried out to live it had a connection, according to what I could perceive, with the experience of a Herculean task that everyone must fulfill before freeing themselves from the strongest ties to earthly matter. In the myth of Hercules, this experience is well described in the Eleventh Labor, in the episode called "Cleansing the Stables." There, Hercules has already lit his own inner lamp, which is the capacity for a being to be guided by the self-conscious energies; thus, by means of altruistic service and the aspiration to attain the superior levels of existence, he perceives that he should take peace to other beings. We know this stage is that where we let go of our own individual entanglements and enter altruistic and group service, that from the moment this light is lit, there is no longer the possibility for anyone to completely return to the darkness they have just left behind. Although sporadically we may find ourselves inside of it, by continual purification one eventually attains complete awakening.

An important moment in the purification process is the discovery of altruism. This discovery is accomplished by degrees and, during the first stages, people offer their free time to work on behalf of others. They also donate, in this beginning, part of the goods that are not needed. As time passes, they give what is in excess from their own budget, and distribute to others that which is superfluous. But this is still not truly useful for the general plan of evolution that, to truly realize itself needs the dedication of the entire being.

And, it is in the course of this whole first phase of purification that the energy of altruism starts to expand within the human being, so that, finally, they agree to set out for the shadowy areas of the consciousness to regenerate them. Then begins for real the task of "cleansing the stables", as described in the history of the myth of Hercules and as my being experienced for many years. It is clear that, upon deciding to do this, human beings are not always understood by their fellow beings on the surface of the Earth, who still live for themselves. Their attitude is even considered strange by them.

In spite of the disbelief of those around them, the individuals who are being purified go into the pestilent world and liberate it from its millenary filth without using force. Intuitively they discover that, by removing the obstacles to general cleansing, the task takes care of itself. However, for this activity to be true and fruitful, they must be totally disinterested in any result that their work in this world might bring them, and they must try to maintain themselves attuned with their own superior levels of consciousness.

Thus, they discover in this first stage of purification (that is developed through the course of several lives on Earth), that it is by the elimination of obstacles that we make possible something real to be built, thus enabling in this way the manifestation of creative work – work that is not personal, but that is done by a higher intelligence. For the readers who feel the necessity to better understand the evolutionary point that the Eleventh Labor of Hercules represents, I have excerpted in the Appendix (see page 137 of this book a selection from the work TIME FOR INNER GROWTH – *The Myth of Hercules Today*). There this description of the trajectory of a man who passed from personal purification to the service to the world is described, the course of the man who made himself useful to the Plan of Evolution. From then on, he enters the next phases of purification.

The second stage of spiritual purification brings the knowledge of cosmic laws, which is a result of the previous stage, described in the penultimate labor of Hercules. The pleiad affirmed that the inner being that was liberated and now finds itself in supraphysical worlds is going through an apprenticeship process that is incomprehensible to those living the earthly life. For my part, I feel reflections of what is happening "there", and I notice my inner feelings expanding themselves, without my doing anything for this to happen. There is something growing light-years away.

The pleiad also confirmed for me what I had been perceiving: that the inner being who occupies the body that is writing this book "knows" laws that it will gradually transmit to my physical brain. At cyclically determined moments, when the circumstances are prepared and the need is real, these laws will be disclosed.

For the time being, this garment must live experiences of purification on different levels, totally protected, controlled and guided, whether inwardly, whether by the external circumstances that surround it. Obedience is necessary in this delicate stage, and these words I am using, "totally protected, controlled and guided," are exact to express this state.

The pleiad affirms that the monadic transmutation, that is, the substitution of one inner being for another, has nothing to do with the phenomenon of incorporation of an entity. As an intergalactic consciousness and as a being in charge of helping the process of subtilizing the Earth, he asserts that any incorporation is considered an obsolete stage in relation to the New Human Being. I was able to establish this in the contact with Ashtar Asghran, previously described; I never had the awareness of being "incorporated" by this being in the way it is generally described in the known technical books, but I was aware of being united with him.

With regard to this, I was present in moments when the pleiad was in contact with other galaxies, receiving information about the current situation of planet Earth, while, at the same time, he talked to me. I perceived that it happened and that he was able to give equal attention to both areas of communication.

Therefore, that which the most advanced instructors of the past cycle said with respect to the inadequacy of any and all attachment to phenomena, such as that of incorporation or of certain transmissions that alter the external state of ordinary human beings, can be considered a basic and precursor teaching for the current evolutionary stage.

The third stage of purification begins when a person frees themselves from the idea of death. I knew I had freed myself of this idea when I saw that the inner being that had vivified this garment for fifty and eight years had gone away without even giving a sign of what it was doing. This was perhaps the greatest joy that this garment has ever felt in all its life: to know that an inner spiritual essence had liberated itself from the limitations of dense matter, entering into other supraphysical laws. Now this garment is occupied by the being that is here, another monad of the one cosmic being that I am; [18]and as long as this being's task on Earth lasts, this body will be working, within the law of service. If, when this task ends, this garment can still be useful, according to cosmic will and within a superior plan (that includes the group of my seven monads), it may eventually be occupied by another inner being; however, this does not happen in an indiscriminate way, but within supraphysical and superior laws that are known by the monads included in the process – laws that will be in effect in the coming cycle of the Earth. Thus instructing me, the pleiad pointed to my external figure. As long as it can be a good instrument, "It can serve the Hierarchy of the inner beings." Being more purified than now, this garment will be more useful and it will have lived well, will have served and it will demand less for its own subsistence. This is the education through

---

[18] The Regent-Avatar is the real individual, the deepest nucleus of the being's consciousness. It expresses itself through the seven monads. For more information, see UNVEILED SECRETS (*Iberah and Anu Tea*) and THE BIRTH OF THE FUTURE HUMANITY.

which an external body passes while it serves as instrument for the monads that inhabit it.

Now I could understand what Helena Blavatsky wanted to say when, in Volume VI of THE SECRET DOCTRINE,[19] she referred to "the multiple nature and the various aspects of the human monad" and, in order not to leave any doubt about the type of transmutation described here, I must add that the physical bodies that are suitable for these monadic changes are already bodies that are well disciplined and controlled and that, therefore, can collaborate without great resistance with the tasks that the new inner being must carry out.

The fourth stage is connected to the liberation of the being from the law of physical birth, in the way that it expresses itself on the surface of the Earth today. The experience of birth through the normal process is painful for the incarnating inner self, and this is a condition to be transcended by humanity in general.

The mutation that occurred in this process is identical in the liberation from the law of death and in

---
[19] Editoria Pensamento.

the liberation from the law of birth; everything happens without pain: with love. Within the new laws, there is full knowledge of what happens, both in the act of leaving oneself from the physical body, in the case of the "being that departs", and in the act of entering this same body, in the case of the "being now in service". The first enters the subtle world, and the second one comes to the material world. Both have full knowledge of everything that happens, approve of the change and work together—one taking with it the inner body, the other taking on a dense body to accomplish the task that is before it.

The being that left this body and now finds itself on supraphysical levels on a planet that is considered distant according to ordinary spatial laws, is, at this moment, learning to free itself forever from the law of physical birth. In other material and corporeal worlds, it could create its own vehicle of manifestation without passing through birth as it is known here; and, if one day it returns to the Earth, it will no longer need this garment or neither the permanent atom[20] that this material garment carries with it. My inner being allows me to notice all this because, since the time this garment was the body of a child,

---

[20] In Esoteric Psychology, the permanent atom is the nucleus that synthesizes all previous experience of the being in a certain material level, and acts as seed for the creation of new bodies, in the next incarnations.

it knew that all this experience of being born and of dying was about to end; but, with its limited brain, it interpreted it in another manner, influenced as it was by the myths, by the superstitions and by the human imagination. Now, however, this garment knows that it can have different destinies: it can be turned over to another inner being, that can and needs to occupy it; its physical, emotional and mental atoms can be restored to the general repository of this planet's atoms; it can be transferred during the coming global operation prepared by the space vessels for the benefit of planet Earth and the rescueable humanity from its surface; or it can live in ERKS, in Brotherhood.

This personality was trained to not create expectations. Whatever destiny these bodies may have, it will be fine with it. With all its strength, the outer garment also says "yes" to its Creator and accepts the higher will.

Part Three

The New Life

*"For him, the realm of death
no longer exists."*

Taking on the new contacts

My conscious self began to ask itself what its next "Labor of Hercules" would be, now that it found itself occupied by an inner being that had been on an incorporeal level for more than two thousand years. The answer could be given to it because the external garment was surrendered to the superior will and would not hesitate before that which would be revealed in this regard, whatever it might be.

The first revelation was for testing the emotional and mental bodies and was followed by instructions that, in a very recent past, this garment would have found difficult to accept and carry out. The passing of the test served to establish some stages to be carried out and they are going to be presented here as a reference for those students who seek transformation through the law of purification, a law that will be very active on Earth in these times.

In this cycle (or in a coming stage of the Earth), the parts to be accomplished as planetary service were presented to me in a certain order to facilitate understanding; nevertheless, at the same time that they are successive, they are concurrent and follow the law of necessity. Here they are, according to how they were received.[21]

Stage of Philosophical-Religious Teaching

This inner being will give instruction about the origin of the inhabitants of the surface of the Earth to those who otherwise ignore it. There are evolutionary phases in the law of creation and involutionary phases, and the students who are receptive to transformation must be taught about them, so that they may go through them harmoniously and without deviation. The direct path is advisable when one knows the law that the being must carry out.

In this stage is included information about the changes that take place in the Hierarchies who are the governors of this planet, so that the humanity of the surface may distinguish clearly the energies that rule it in each world period.

---

[21] The books by Trigueirinho published after this one (see list on pg. 147) portray the development of these stages.

The religious philosophy that is supposed to shine on Earth includes the knowledge of the existence of the Space Gardeners, in charge of the introduction of the new genetic code in the race of the surface[22]. If the individuals are attuned with this work, the Space Gardeners may take their bodies to non-material planes or to the vessels, where changes can implement themselves (as has happened with me), both from the point of view of purification and harmonization of the subtle bodies (as I lived during the first nights in the Valley of ERKS) and, also, from the point of view of transmutation (that I experienced later and which allowed the inner being who had fulfilled its mission to become liberated and to transmigrate from this Earth to another world).

Before 8/8/88, the Space Gardeners took care of the races in the sense of controlling the evolutionary behavior on the surface of the Earth so that, for example, they would not subject to excessively strenuous efforts during primitive times, and during others.

After 8/8/88, these cosmic beings started working together with the race of the surface changing their genetic code. The new code brings the elements that will

---

[22] See THE SPACE GARDENERS and THE NEW BEGINNING OF THE WORLD.

permit terrestrials to live in harmony, ignoring the aggressive laws they have adopted until now. Thus, planet Earth will become part of the Intergalactic Councils.

Cultural Stage

The new culture to be manifested on the surface of the Earth after the global purification will bring unheard of knowledge about higher laws of astronomy and physics. It is necessary to transcend the point where we currently find these sciences, where we have still not distinguished the difference between a star and a vessel, or between a planet and a satellite created by supraphysical civilizations. In this cultural stage, there will be a period of preparation to master all the laws that are to be revealed to the humanity of the surface.

Scientific Stage

This stage will set the patterns of life for the inhabitants of the surface of the Earth, patterns that will not be created by the mind or by habits, but by knowledge of the new laws. These laws should really be applied in life by humanity, and it is this that will receive the name of the scientific stage. It refers to intuitively receiving the laws and living them, so that it will no longer be necessary to conduct stressful "scientific" experiments, thus avoiding disharmony between humanity and Nature, and between the various levels of the human being itself.

Stage of Knowledge of Natural Laws

During this stage, as a principle, there will be no aggression to Nature. Thus the knowledge of the laws of supra-nature, which are immaterial, will begin to disclose themselves to humanity. Knowing these laws, humanity will control the rain, the winds, and the weather in general and will command, in an intelligent way (and not selfishly) the waters and the telluric movements.

Stage of Knowledge and of Education for Objective Life

This stage will take into account that education is not to be based on syncretism or on the experiences of others. Education will have the goal of manifesting a spiritual life within the cosmic law, and not to shape people according to the current models. Today, human beings are educated to be useful to a sick society and outside of the universal law. It will happen that, in the future, that which will be offered as education will be the awakening and manifestation of the inner being according to directives transmitted by the monad, the cosmic aspect of its life. To work within education and to express the ruling laws of this sector, one must have utmost respect for what is expressed by our fellow beings and the absence of expectations and of previously known schemes. Beings renew themselves constantly, and, therefore, the school for life can no longer be based on the transmission of former experiences, no matter how good they may be. Education will always be new, as the manifestation of a being not conditioned by desire is always new.

Stage of Changes in Structural Patterns

For this stage to develop it may be necessary to implant, on the physical plane, a center of creative life, of harmonization with the external environment, of spiritual life and purification. Thus, the patterns of earthly life may be changed, even if this can only be done to a certain point on the material level before the planetary purification. All the seeds that can today be sown in humanity's inner world, will sprout in a next cycle, when the surface of the Earth has already been transformed.

Stage of Harmonious Integration with the One Life

This seventh stage results from the experience of those previous. It will be realized as a result of the presence on Earth of beings and entities who come from pleiades where all the stages here described have been overcome. These beings, who will be among humanity of the surface, will radiate their energy and demonstrate, through their own example, that which the human terrestrial race can manifest without expending energy on experiences that, once free will has been transcended, are considered superfluous. There will be an experience of unity with cosmic beings after the change in the material and subtle constitution of humanity. The experience of mental unity will be a fact between individuals in the future cycle of this planet.

The degree of the whole Earth's density will pass through great changes, permitting the expression of a spiritual life less influenced by the illusion of the world than it is today. The new genetic code will bring a transformation in the thinking state and the amount of liquid in the physical body will be considerably reduced. New species of plants and minerals will enable adequate physical nourishment without solid products, and aggressiveness, currently considered normal, will be completely excluded from human life.

Humanity of the surface of the Earth has a lower self and a higher self, although it is not always mentally aware of this. The lower self is the part of the being that normally uses the left-side consciousness[23] to express itself, and which manifests violence and aggressiveness; the higher self acts by means of the right-side consciousness, with access to the evolutionary law of the races and to a philosophy that leads it to the unknown, without fears or resistances.

Moreover, the human being is also a monad on the cosmic plane. In general, because they only have awareness of living on a specific planet, members of the race will be able to know only one monad of their "total being". In reality, however, the human being constitutes itself of seven monads, each one of them destined for experiences in different worlds. Awareness of this fact may, in the future, be given to humankind, when it enters into the process of unification with its deepest nucleus[24]. Therefore, above these seven monads, there is within the constitution of the being that which is called the Cosmic Man[25], which does not involve itself in experiences of the material universe, but only sees, in a perfect way, the Plan that it participates in. It is not possible to

---

[23] The left-side consciousness is linked to analysis, to deduction and to logic; therefore, it is circumscribed to that which it knows, to individual and collective past and to free will.

[24] See THE BIRTH OF THE FUTURE HUMANITY.

[25] Also called monadic Regent or Eighth Monad.

describe such a reality with ordinary language. Even the Irdin language, used by the intergalactic beings when they communicate through sounds, is unable to express certain higher states.

"So be it. You have chosen. Due to your own decision you can no longer regress", the priests of past secret societies would say. Today, the intergalactic beings say nothing and we seek no intellectual explanations for the Mystery. This Mystery, therefore, brings itself so close that:

"Without ever having looked through the window, we can see the Way to Heaven."

The whole process of evolution already reflects itself in the human soul as the goal of humanity. Thus, a person has the ability to consciously receive the Teaching, while in the past it needed to have its physical nature completely paralyzed for this to happen, as related in the chronicles of the ancient Mystery Schools. Today the Teaching is transmitted while one remains awake and in perfect harmony.

Thus happened the experience that I was able to live in the Valley of ERKS.

The three requests

The experience seemed to be finished when the pleiad, receiving an inner communication from the space vessels that were visibly present there, told me I could make three requests—but it could not be for material things. I had at that moment the confirmation that such things do not count for the genuine process of ascesis that leads us to the incorporeal worlds. I understood "to be in the world but not of the world" described by Jesus, the Christ, and I saw very clearly that the integration of an individual into the immaterial plane should be the most intimate and complete possible.

Although I had the habit to not request anything from the higher energies, because I always had as a certainty that God knows our needs better than we do, I saw that the offer from those "gods" who, at that moment, were to be found in the space vessels, was an opportunity, one more grace that was flowing. So I made these three requests: the first one, not to be turned down for service to the Evolutionary Plan; the second one, that all who were on the Path with me, evolve together; and the third one, that the light and love of the cosmic beings always be present while I am working for the Plan.

In addition, the pleiad confirmed that the inner being that was now within this human garment was one of the monads of the Cosmic Man that I am, that Cosmic Man who is above all the subdivisions of the human constitution. He also informed me that the inner being that had since departed from this garment was another monad of this same Essence.

According to the pleiad, the teaching about the existence of the seven monads ruled by the Cosmic Man is now basic for the correct comprehension of the human beings' constitution and its experiences of transmigration. Until now, this constitution had been presented to humanity of the surface in a simplified form, due to its limited intellectual coefficient; but with the new genetic code, the human being will be able to enter another phase of its learning.

This deep inner essence, the Cosmic Man which we are, manifests itself through seven monads, as we have already said. Each one of them is capable of having a certain type of experience, on many planets or on various levels of manifestation. Everything is decided by this essence on the cosmic plane, following and fulfilling the law of evolution. This essence has a "cosmic name", which it is given at the moment of its creation, in the beginning of times. It was what I heard, in my experience. It is for me, an energy in motion.

The Cosmic Man, therefore, projects the seven monads on different planes, because through these extensions, it will be able to contact concrete and subtle planes and thus live its experiences. The eighth nucleus, that of the essence itself, is beyond these necessities. There are millions of planets, on the most diverse levels, that are habitable worlds. Each monad, within the evolutionary law, has a period of time to transform itself into a perfect individual. The Eighth Monad – or the Cosmic Essence, or the Cosmic Man – has also been called the Father, through the times[26].

As much as the physical, so also the emotional and the mental bodies must evolve during the cycles of manifestation of the monad that inhabits them.

---

[26] Concerning the evolution of the monads, see UNVEILED SECRETS *(Iberah and Anu Tea)*

When they have attained the maximum progress possible in a certain stage, their essence is absorbed by higher nuclei of the being. The monad then lives in its own body that is infinitely more subtle than the terrestrial bodies and incomprehensible to the ordinary mind of today.

The life of these earthly bodies takes place in the world of appearances, while the life of the monads is found on levels beyond illusions. The Father, or Cosmic Essence, imprints his characteristics in them, full of cosmic vibration and universal rhythms. The incarnations occur within the law of evolution, which is introduced in different degrees – from the material karmic law to other circumvolutions, more free and conscious, of higher planes. The seven monads of the same Father live their experiences concurrently, on different planets and, one of them may also enter, cyclically, into a life more full of divinity.

Human beings can have consciousness of these monads as they fulfill their cycles and evolve through service. At this moment, for example, I know that two of the seven monads that I am are each living on different planes, although they are close to each other in evolution. One is in this human garment that is writing, and the other is in an incorporeal world, as I have mentioned. With regard to the other ones, I still do not have conscious understanding of them.

The Cosmic Essence, also called the Eighth Monad (called "the eighth chakra" in certain hermetic Eastern orders of the past), awaits its cyclical time to proceed freely as Avatar. The Eighth Monad of every human being is an Avatar. When an Avatar is among us, on the physical plane or on subtle ones, this means that the Eighth Monad is completing its time of creation. This is why an Avatar is sacred. It is not seven monads, each one fulfilling its task, but a single Eighth Monad in its final process and in preparation for something that the human mind is not able to conceive.

That same night I learned that this human garment I carry had been prepared for twenty-five years for these experiences in the Valley of ERKS, and for the new tasks that it is now being given. I realized in only one glimpse what had been the life of this garment in all these years of the earthly calendar. The rhythms, the cycles it went through, were perfectly controlled and a new stage begins itself now. The concepts that this garment had, that it carried imprinted in itself about these inner movements, have lost their value today. I now notice the presence of another "control", to which I surrender the best way I can.

That which, as a monad waits for me in the coming times, on the surface of this planet or in intraterrestrial worlds, begins to be clear to me, as well as the possibilities arising from certain optional situations appearing. While the pleiad was giving me this information and while, together, we checked the topics of the books we still had to write ("if there is time," he always added), I noticed that our lives have no other meaning but service, given that humanity from the surface of the Earth has little time left to receive the basic information it needs so much during this period of purification.

Since planet Earth will live laws of universal character, the humanity of the surface must inform itself about what is possible regarding the new circumstances that are approaching, so that the process of transition may be harmonious and so that each person may transform themselves into a cooperator of the Great Plan. One's harmonious attitude in the face of events to come will be of great value to the Earth, to the solar system and to all the worlds connected with this one. Each one of us is potentially, therefore, an important part within a greater work.

Until recently, we have been preparing humanity and the planet for the great transition prescribed in the Plan of Evolution. In those periods, the spiritual teaching was directed to character building, to alignment of the personality with the higher self and to psychological strengthening of individuals, regarding the changes that were happening in increasing rhythm. This stage of preparation, however, has already been transcended; we are now living great changes. This new phase which we have entered implies deep transformation, purification and preparation for the construction of structures and of patterns that are totally different from the known, compatible exclusively with the coming cycle of humanity and of the planet. Therefore, from now on our service will be primarily to provide information that is practical, necessary and adequate for the new times. The work is the same, but has entered a new phase. In other words, it has been brought up to date.

A transformation in laws is taking place in all planes of the terrestrial sphere, as if an improvement of each one of them were being consummated. The movements of planetary transiting and rotation, for example, as well as the atmospheric pressure, alters itself in harmony with the changes of the other stars, each one within its own laws and in conformity with higher laws. The Earth turns itself less dense, and this is an influence on everything that exists on it. That part of humanity which chose to participate in this change is experiencing transformations that are reflected even in their physical bodies.

The persons who intuitively perceive that there are micro-organs implanted inside certain organs of their body can clearly see why they undergo unexpected healing and enjoy good health. Those who need treatment may even be carried to other planes of life, where they are aided by surgical operations, with perceptible results on the dense physical body[27].

As the Earth becomes less solid, the non-material laws will begin to rule the life of humanity of the surface. There is a transforming impulse that is affecting the cardiac area of the incarnate beings, because this area is the most directly subject to change in atmospheric pressure. Another area of the physical body that is a priority in this process of transformation is the kidney area, so that the individuals may have better conditions to purify themselves and to eliminate the toxins accumulated during the cycles of ignorance and blindness. Finally, the digestive area is also a priority, so that the acceptance, assimilation and transformation of food may take

---

[27] See MIRNA JAD—Inner Sanctuary.

place according to new nutritional situations, no longer based solely on material products and their physical properties.

With the changes that have already begun to occur in humanity, and with the global purification of the surface of the Earth, new plant species will appear. On the other hand, the minerals that have contributed to the present destruction of planetary life, such as uranium, for example, and the plants that contribute to chaos, such as the tobacco plant and those used to produce drugs, will be removed from the terrestrial orbit.

Bloodthirsty animals will also end their cycles of life on Earth. Those who will remain, or who will be brought back here, are those who will have the ability to collaborate with the new humanity and to evolve with it. As we have already seen, this new human being will not be aggressive. Therefore humanity will coexist with some animals, helping them to progress. It will not act as now when it uses the animals without the intention of rendering service to them.

A new diet will appear, free from today's habits. It will not include solid products that require the canine, premolar and molar teeth; all the dentition will be made up of incisor teeth, because fruits and cereals, after the purification of the surface of the planet, will be different. Humanity will also count on immaterial means of subsistence provided by the Ono-Zone energy, present everywhere in the universe.

The individuals who feel the need for a new world and a new life are already engaged with this transformation; they will have the outer and inner help they need to pass through the transition. It is no longer required to live in isolation in order for the union with the spiritual life to take place.

Even if, for now they are surrounded by a collective psychosis (such as the one that characterizes humanity's present life) and in direct contact with matters on the human level, such union may occur, because the obstacles to inner realization are not outside, but are within ourselves.

The new being, who has spiritual consciousness, transmutes itself in its collective action, in which other beings and their own parts are integrated: one of these parts is controlled by the left side consciousness and the other one by the right-side consciousness, which now awakens.

The ancient wisdom affirmed:

"This is the Way to Heaven."
And its question came right after:
"When the gates of Heaven open or close, will we be able to carry out the feminine role?"

What role is this? Wouldn't it be for us to enter a more receptive condition and, consequently, take on more creative functions?

To participate in the intergalactic journey

By a being from ERKS:

The initiatory Journey will be physical.

The Guides and the monads will take you with their resources and science, with love and generosity.

For you to know how to guide other terrestrial brothers and sisters, the general outline will be given to you right after you begin the tasks. Before that, you will pass through a period of inner instruction, developed through your own Guide or your own monad.

The brothers from space will be with you, in the heart, and this state will persist for a long time.

Periods of trial on Earth will come for all beings, from all the kingdoms and of all the races. Allow cosmic love to rest in your heart, in the light that penetrates you. It is necessary, however, that you let go of the ties you have made through free will; let go of temptation, hatred, and greed. Love is the key to enter the Father's Place.

You will manifest your love for God by loving all, in quietude. Devotion is to be included, and its energy is the door to Omnipresence. You must be willing to serve all souls in need, for this is how the future men and women of this Earth will be formed. Humility and wisdom will be acquired in other spheres of consciousness, with the Presence and in silence. On the cosmic planes there are ripe fruits for those who love in this way.

In ERKS is the source that nourishes the awakening. You will find me beside you in all the circumstances, and you will know of me in silence; you will hear my voice within you and you will see my face, whose image will reach you through your awakened intellect.

You will know, then, how to go on without my help, but I will be waiting for you until you arrive. I will not leave without you, because I have come to get you. This is why I led you to the encounter, in silence and with love. I will not allow you to wander, lost and helpless, on paths that are still unknown. In the eternal cosmic love I will fetch you, without a visible sign and without audible sound. My envoys have reached you through several visits and have joined you to others; afterwards, I gathered you all and now I speak to you directly.

We will return from these contacts with new experiences, with greater desire to serve, and we will wait for the next awakening. Then your heart, now tired, will dream, until it merges itself with the human transformation, because there is an inner change we seek for all.

In the new sphere of consciousness the mother-energy nourishes you without ceasing, so that you have enough strength to follow me. You will know, then, the immortal Son who was forged in love. As we do with you now, you will do with others.

With all your love you will love those who do not love you, together with those who love you with unselfish love. All souls will come to you. In the ocean of love you will contact the members of Our Brotherhood, and you will teach the creatures that the Father loves with equality all your fellow brothers and sisters.

I will answer your call, gently merging you with the light of my vehicle; I will take away your sadness and you will feel, then, the way that the mystical light embraces you in silence and merges itself with your body. I will cross all the hills with my light and I will come to meet you forever.

You will contemplate, in silence, in a nocturnal space, until the day arrives; then you will get accustomed to waiting for me, until we become united in the same harmony of love.

You will keep your eyes fixed inwardly and you will no longer need to seek me, because I will reach you and we will travel to the stars that answer us with their light.

Send me the radiation of your thoughts. The Mirrors will reflect you and tell you what you are, because there is no space between your mind and mine.

Appendix

The law of transmutation

The expression of patterns of behavior that are higher than what is habitual always involves the law of transmutation – a law that acts through the flow of the fiery current of life-power and also through the magnetism of a higher nucleus that serves as a pole of attraction for the substances that must be elevated. In many cases this law works directly on the core of the particles and of the consciousnesses of the living beings, so as to expel from them the forces that can prevent the fulfillment of the Evolutionary Plan.

This term, *transmutation*, has been used on very different levels, among which we can point out:

• material transmutation (individual or group), which is the raising of the energy from the physical-etheric or mental-emotional planes;

- monadic transmutation, in which the monad that occupies a certain vehicle gives it to another, more evolved, thus going through the experience of being liberated from the law of death;

- logoic transmutation, which is when the regent nucleus of a universe is changed.

In all these cases, transmutation is an important energetic movement that, in the present stage of humanity and of the planet as a whole, requires intense action by the Hierarchies.

Transmutation of Energies or Material Transmutation[28]

Since ancient times, material transmutation has been an object of great attention on the part of those who seek to serve the higher law. This attention is intensified on Earth because the planet received into its orbit the expurgation of forces from other points of the cosmos. Since every movement of forces in the universe is generated by the law of attraction, this happened also because of the vibratory level presented by this planet and its humanity.

They remained, then, apart from fulfilling the divine purpose. The state of consciousness that they

---
[28] For more information, see THE FORMATION OF HEALERS and TIME FOR HEALING (*The Occult Life*).

found themselves in did not even permit them to have a representative in the Councils directing the galaxy.

On various occasions, the energetic situation on Earth reached such a point of disharmony, chaos and conflict that the planet was on the verge of being destroyed. However, because of the service rendered in freeing other celestial bodies from having to face involutionary situations, the Earth has always received greater assistance on the part of the Hierarchies, in the sense of transmuting the forces that took it to this state.

Transmutation is a law that rules various planes and assumes a different appearance, depending on the need, and there are Hierarchies and Entities that have as a basic task to apply this law to planetary levels. Some deal directly with the matter that constitutes these levels; others deal with the consciousnesses focused on them, and still others radiate emanations of the transmuting fire that, permeating these levels, break loose a selection of the vibrations present there and channel those vibrations that are out of place to the precise levels to which they correspond.

Therefore, in order for the psychic layers of the planet to become more clear, and to maintain the terrestrial magnetic balance of the planet, a permanent work is necessary, because these layers continuously receive the emanations of the collective mental and emotional levels.

With reference to a human being, the transmutation of energies begins when its monad awakens to cosmic reality, a reality that corresponds to the vibration of its own level of existence. This recognition promotes in the being's outer consciousness an opening to a more elevated life, one which can prepare the matter of its bodies to receive the impulses and energetic currents that will take it to a subtler form of expression – which is a phase that comes before ascesis.

The attainment of the successive stages of this process leads humanity to liberate itself from the semi-primitive stage in which it finds itself and to express the more sublime facets of its being. Such a process – represented in alchemy by the transformation of lead into gold – requires the intervention of an instrument called the "philosopher's stone". Among the attributes that lead humans to encounter this instrument is a basic one: the control of the forces that, in desires and thoughts, enslave them to the world of forms.

This control lies latent within one's own being, and the vivification and dynamization of this dormant potential counts on the help of high Hierarchies and Entities that watch its journey on the paths that lead to truth.

Thus, the purification and transformation of the inferior aspects of the individual do not occur only through the monadic impulse. Hierarchies, healers, consciousnesses and supraphysical energies help in this process that, to be finished, depends on the change of the genetic code of the beings who will repopulate the Earth after the holocaust that is approaching.

Material transmutation requires a considerable degree of liberation from the ties with matter and, to fully accomplish itself, should receive greater collaboration from the humanity of the surface; however, the commitment that humans maintain to the illusory levels of existence does not permit it to occur easily.

The involutionary forces are impregnated in the particles of the material planes of the Earth, and every being that inhabits this planet receives a great part of these forces into their bodies. The degree of the involvement that a kingdom has with these forces determines the percentage of their infiltration in its components.

The human kingdom is one of those that carry the largest amount and, like the planet, receives special attention from healing energies in order to transmute the matter of its bodies, to elevate its vibration and to enable it to recognize the spiritual path. Without a firm connection with these energies there is no possibility to let oneself be transfigured into the image of the Supreme.

Monadic transmutation[29]

In monadic transmutation, a monad that has already fulfilled its evolutionary stage in one incarnation gives its material bodies to another one which, freed from the law of physical birth and having accepted the law of sacrifice, comes to perform some task on the terrestrial planes. Through this form of service both grow in light and in consciousness. Transmutation can be the access to immaterial worlds.

This process will be broadly active during the next planetary cycle, when humanity is more detached from the concrete planes. It will be one of the normal mechanisms for the incarnation of beings.

Also at the time of rescue and the period of restructuring of the Earth, many monads, through

---

[29] For more information, see THE BOOK OF SIGNS.

transmutation, will hand-over their bodies to higher beings, which will thus be able to work more directly in the dense layers.

Logoic transmutation[30]

The substitution of the ruling consciousness of a universe, be it planetary or on a wider range, is given the name of logoic transmutation. Little is known about the details involved in this substitution, due to its profoundness; however, we can say it is always followed by great changes in all levels of existence of the universe in question.

Transmutation and the fires[31]

Sublimation occurs in the outer layers of the particles, purifying them; elevating that which is volatile to bring them to a more subtle state, free from impurities. Transmutation, rather, occurs in the essence, modifies the nature of the particles: they take the being from where it is so that it can bring itself to another reality, even though they may remain in

---

[30] For more information see UNVEILED SECRETS *(Iberah and Anu Tea)* and CREATION (In the Paths of Energy).

[31] Based on the book NEW ORACLES by Trigueirinho.

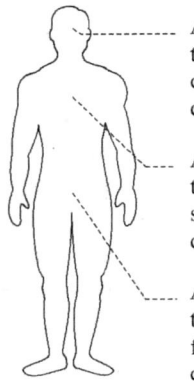

- Area in which the aspects of cosmic fire are concentrated
- Area in which the aspects of solar fire are concentrated
- Area in which the aspects of fricative fire are concentrated

the original solid state. Sublimation may be achieved through fire by friction[32], whereas transmutation requires impulses that only more potent fires are capable of providing.

Although the areas of the bodies have various fires active in different proportions, the bodies as a whole emit a vibration in a specific frequency that depends on the energetic level reached by the being's consciousness; in other words, it depends on the position of the being on the initiatic scale.

In the beginning of this ascent the sublimation and transmutation of energies occurs in an indirect way and almost always during sleep. In more advanced phases, the processes of sublimation intensify themselves; in addition to participating more in them, the consciousness of the being starts to recognize the transmuting action of solar fire.

---

[32] The fires, energies that animate the universes, have natural and supranatural aspects. Fire by friction, proper to dense matter, is natural and intrinsic to all that exists in the outer world. The electric and cosmic fires, also found in all beings, are supra-natural and, for them to manifest themselves, one has to establish attunement with transcendent vibrations. The fire by friction is already expressed in humankind, while supra-natural fires exist as a promise, and act in the outer world when, through love, its consciousness ascends to spiritual levels.

As the fire by friction is capable of promoting sublimation, the solar fire is capable of carrying out transmutation. Nevertheless, this does not mean that every action of the solar fire results in a transmutation as it can also bring the being to sublimation. On the other hand, at the core of the cosmic fire is the secret to materialization and dematerialization. The transmuting energy also encompasses the level in which exist the forces that permit the cohesion of a particle, but is not able to neutralize all of them. Only the cosmic fire reaches this level of action. The materialization and dematerialization is exactly what the energy of fire sets in motion with regard to the cosmic register, where exists the parameters for the dissipation and construction of the bodies.

These processes are thus being presented and highlighted so that we may understand them. All the fires will participate in everything that happens, varying the proportion of their action in each case. The more unified their action is, the more it will awaken the subtle centers of the bodies.

These subtle centers are vortices, almost always latent, destined for supraluminary contact and for the manifestation of life in rhythms that transcend those of the pulsation of light. Their vibration projects itself in an area above the head, in the energetic aura that goes beyond the limits of a being's physical body. In them are the seeds of cosmic communion— a stage of broader relationship that awaits humanity of today.

Cleansing the stables

With regard to the process of purification that we are addressing, we here excerpt a chapter of the book TIME FOR INNER GROWTH (*The Myth of Hercules Today*)[33]:

Hercules now lives an experience that determines a great and final change in his life. Having lit in himself his own lamp through altruistic service and alignment with higher levels of his consciousness, he must take this light to other beings. Those who follow his evolution are very attentive to his development, because from the moment that this light is lit, one does not have the opportunity to return to complete illusion. From now on, Hercules will be a conscious co-creator, and it will not be possible for him to return to his internal motivation.

He is, therefore, called to seek an encounter with a "beacon", and not a tiny wavering light anymore. This

---

[33] By the same author, Editora Pensamento.

beacon, which is also inside of him, is part of the same light, but introduces many fewer veils. Hercules must now change the direction of his steps; instead of paying so much attention to himself, he must turn his back on what he has built and meet those who walk in darkness, those who have not yet lit their own lamp.

The Instructor, then, proposes to him that he go to the kingdom of Augeas, a territory that needs to be cleansed of an ancestral evil.

As Hercules sets out for there, an unbearable stench becomes perceptible. The immense region where Augeas is king symbolizes the sense of property, ingrained in humans since times immemorial.

This kingdom has existed for ages, and its stench comes from the excrement accumulated for centuries and centuries. During all this time in which the cattle defecated in the stables, there has never been any cleaning. Also the ancient fields, originally intended for agriculture, are completely covered by manure and no vegetation is possible there. There is so much manure piled up in this great property of Augeas, that an epidemic is starting to spread itself on the whole kingdom, decimating hundreds of human lives.

Hercules proceeds to the king's palace. "I am the owner of everything", Augeas says to him, as soon as he sees

Hercules before him. "I have always been the owner, and in these lands only what I permit is allowed." The hero does not inspire confidence in him, mainly because he is not asking for any reward for the job he proposes to do.

"Only an incompetent person would be willing to clean the stables of my property without receiving any reward", he affirms. Not minding what the sovereign's says, Hercules calmly insists on doing the task.

"Very well," says the king, "I do not trust those who say they are detached. You must have a hidden plan; you must be an astute person who aims at usurping my kingdom, my land and my cattle. In truth, what you really want is my throne. It is about a game of power. But, in the end I will make a concession and let you work here."

The king had never heard anyone speak of people who try to serve the world without seeking any benefit. To him, a great landowner, this was a novelty, but the necessity of cleansing was so great that he said he would accept the presence of any idiot willing to do it.

He then proposes a deal with Hercules, because, according to him, "I would be demoralized if I did not take precautions against such an eccentric adventurer." Not to be criticized by his millions of subjects and not to be considered a foolish king, he proposes that the warrior clean all the stables in only one day. "If you do this, you will receive a tenth of my enormous herd, but, if you fail you will be killed," he affirmed.

The warrior accepts.

Hercules leaves the king with his disbelief and walks for a while around the fetid and pestilent lands. Carts go by him, carrying piles of corpses, victims of the epidemic and of the generalized filth. A little longer and the whole world would be caught up in this environment of death. It is necessary, therefore, to prevent this immediately. Hercules closes his eyes and tries to concentrate himself. Minutes later, when he opens them, he notices that there are two rivers flowing calmly nearby. Standing on the bank, he watches the waters go by. Then, to his mind, from the high levels of his consciousness comes a clear, definitive idea: that of redirecting the course of the rivers, which can be done in a few hours, and let the water run through the stables. The torrents, while they flow, will take with them all the filth of the feces accumulated for centuries.

And so he does: he diverts the water flow and watches as they assist in cleaning the land. In a short time the kingdom is washed, and in only one day—according to the agreement with the king — the task is done. There is now another kind of air to breathe. The land, unobstructed, *begins to create new life. Hercules seeing the result, goes back to the presence of the king.*

Augeas shouts, very aggressively, "It was not you who cleaned the land. Impostor that you are, you employed a trick, using the waters of the rivers that run here to accomplish the task." Completely furious, the king then screams, "You plotted all this in order to endear yourself to my subjects and to steal my throne. Get out of here immediately, if you do not want me to have your head cut off."

Without answering, the warrior leaves. Something tells him the task is done and that he must report to the Beings who preside over all, and not to the ruler of these lands. And so he turns to his Instructor from whom he hears this sentence, "Now you have transformed yourself into a server of the world."[34]

In reality, Hercules had opened himself to intuition, that is, he had used his own light to make the light of others shine. One day this light will shine in everyone, because Augeas, "king of property", does not have eternal life on Earth and the retrograde forces he represents also are temporary, since they carry the seed of their own destruction.

---

[34] **THE LABOURS OF HERCULES**, Alice A. Bailey, Lucis Trust, Geneva – London – New York, 1974.

Some characteristics mark an already evolved being, such as Hercules in this penultimate Labor. Disinterested service is the first of these, and it is done when the consciousness is no longer focused on the human ego, on its pseudo-needs and expectations. Now one works toward meeting the real needs of others. This, however, is done without any feeling of losing something for the benefit of others. No thought or feeling of this kind passes through Hercules; he simply serves, without feeling a loss of anything. There is no effort at all in his giving.

The second characteristic of the being in service of the world is the ability to work in group. In this story, however, at first sight the hero seems to execute his task alone. What then does it signify, to work in group, at the stage of evolution already reached by him? Forgetting himself before the task for the sake of humanity, concentrating himself on the center of his own consciousness; thus he is internally united with all his fellow beings, forming in reality a group. From this consciousness integrated to humanity as a whole flows a special energy, able to move mountains.

The third characteristic is purity, which implies being more aligned with one's own higher levels of consciousness.

The work of a being rendering service does not always seem important in the eyes of others. Generally it has the same character of simplicity as the task of cleansing stables, considered by all to be of lesser importance. Whatever form this work may take (to work in excrement, to bring cleanliness to a place), this service is not aimed at the personal gain of the one doing it, but to the gain of all. Whatever its nature or the level of evolution of the one who does it is, the important things are the life and love used in the task. It is important execute it and, right after, leave the scene, because the results do not belong to the one who serves.

Already initiated in these basic laws that rule the cosmos, Hercules managed to clean the millenary filth stemming from the sense of property without using great effort. Nevertheless, he had to break down some barriers, such as to overcome the walls of skepticism, of attachment and of incomprehension, implicit in the symbol of the king Augeas – and to execute his task serenely, obeying only his own inner light.

It is by eliminating obstacles that we allow something to be built, enabling the appearance of creative work. After this experience Hercules passes through a deep reflection. Now he is ready for services that are even greater in the eyes of God.

PEACE

About Trigueirinho and His Work

Jose Trigueirinho Netto (1931-2018) was born in Sao Paulo, Brazil. He lived in Europe for a number of years, where he maintained contact with individuals who were advanced on the spiritual path, including Paul Brunton.

In his own life he was an example of the teachings that he transmitted through his books and talks about the transcendence and elevation of the human being, the contact with the soul and with even more profound nuclei of the being, impersonal service, and the link with the Spiritual Hierarchies.

One of the fundamental elements of his work is to stimulate the expansion of human consciousness and to liberate it from the bonds that keep it imprisoned to material aspects of existence, both external and internal.

He was the Founder of the Community of Light Figueira (http://www.comunidadefigueira.org.br) and a Founder and member of the Board of Directors of the Fraternity International Humanitarian Federation (www.fraterinternacional) as well as a Co-Founder of the Grace Mercy Order, an ecumenical Christian monastic order. He also was an active collaborator, instructor and spiritual protector of three other communities located in Uruguay, Argentina and Portugal.

In his last 30 years he lived in the Community of Light Figueira, in the interior of Minas Gerais, Brazil, a community that at present has approximately 300 residents and which is visited annually by thousands of collaborators who are members of a larger network of humanitarian services and of spiritual studies that was always guided and followed closely by Trigueirinho.

Thanks to his inestimable instruction and his love for the Kingdoms of Nature and as a result of the exemplary work that he himself implanted in the Figueira community, the Animal, Vegetable and Mineral Kingdoms are the recipients of loving treatment there.

Trigueirinho wrote over 80 books, published

originally in Portuguese, with many of them translated into Spanish, English, French and German. He gave more than 3,000 talks that were recorded live and which are available in CD, with some available in DVD and pen drive.

The primary focus of the first phase of Trigueirinho's work was concerned with self-knowledge, prayer, instruction and spiritual transformation. Following this, he began to transmit information with respect to Universal Life and about the assistance that humanity has from its beginnings received by means of the Intra-terrestrial White Brotherhood which inhabits the Retreats and the Planetary Centers as well as through the Cosmic Brotherhood of the Universe. He provides information about the presence of the Spiritual Hierarchy on the planet and the advent of the new humanity.

His work also includes themes relating to: the need for humanity to balance the negative karmas that it has created in relation to the Kingdoms of Nature; the negative karmic burden that we carry from the history of slavery and the genocide of indigenous peoples; and the nature of spiritual work in groups. He also addresses issues of healing, a larger vision of astrology, the esoteric nature of symbols, sound and colors, and the divine feminine.

In his last eight years he analyzed with clarity and with the wisdom that always characterized him, the messages that the Divinity has been giving to the planet as a warning to humanity (available from www.mensajerosdivinos.org/en).

His work reveals a real comprehension of the significance of all the Kingdoms of Nature on our planet, the true spiritual task of the human being, its place in the universe and also its responsibility before Creation.

Finally, he clarifies the reasons for the crisis that today is devastating humanity, teaching how to avoid reacting negatively to an immanent natural catastrophe by contacting more subtle levels of consciousness, and opening perspectives for the beginning of a more luminous cycle for our race.

Books by Trigueirinho

(Books available in English have English title first)

Published by Editora Pensamento
Sao Paulo, Brazil

1987

NOSSA VIDA NOS SONHOS
OUR LIFE IN DREAMS

A ENERGIA DOS RAIOS EM NOSSA VIDA
THE ENERGY OF THE RAYS IN OUR LIVES

1988

DO IRREAL AO REAL
FROM THE UNREAL TO THE REAL

HORA DE CRESCER INTERIORMENTE
O Mito de Hércules Hoje
TIME FOR INNER GROWTH – *The Myth of Hercules Today*

A MORTE SEM MEDO E SEM CULPA
DEATH WITHOUT FEAR AND WITHOUT GUILT

CAMINHOS PARA A CURA INTERIOR
PATHS TO INNER HEALING

1989

ERKS – *Mundo Interno*
ERKS – *The Inner World*

Miz Tli Tlan – *Um Mundo que Desperta*
MIZ TLI TLAN – *A World that Awakens*

Aurora – Essência Cósmica Curadora
AURORA – *Cosmic Essence of Healing*

Signs of Contact
SINAIS DE CONTATO

O Novo Começo do Mundo
THE NEW BEGINNING OF THE WORLD

A Quinta Raça
THE FIFTH RACE

Padrões de conduta para a nova Humanidade
PATTERNS OF CONDUCT FOR THE NEW HUMANITY

Novos Sinais de Contato
NEW SIGNS OF CONTACT

Os Jardineiros do Espaço
THE SPACE GARDENERS

1990

A Busca da Síntese
THE SEARCH FOR SYNTHESIS

Noah's Vessel
A NAVE DE NOÉ

TEMPO DE RETIRO E TEMPO DE VIGÍLIA
A TIME OF RETREAT AND A TIME OF VIGIL

1991

PORTAS DO COSMOS
GATEWAYS OF THE COSMOS

ENCONTRO INTERNO – *A Consciência-Nave*
INNER ENCOUNTER – *The Consciousness Space Vessel*

A HORA DO RESGATE
THE TIME OF RESCUE

O LIVRO DOS SINAIS
THE BOOK OF SIGNS

MIRNA JAD – *Santuário Interior*
MIRNA JAD – *Inner Sanctuary*

AS CHAVES DE OURO
THE GOLDEN KEYS

1992

DAS LUTAS À PAZ
FROM STRUGGLE TO PEACE

A MORADA DOS ELISÍOS
THE ELYSIAN DWELLING PLACE

HORA DE CURAR – *A Existência Oculta*
TIME FOR HEALING – *The Occult Existence*

O RESSURGIMENTO DE FÁTIMA LIS
THE RESURGENCE OF FATIMA LIS

História Escrita nos Espelhos
Princípios de Comunicação Cósmic
HISTORY WRITTEN IN THE MIRRORS -
Principles of Cosmic Communication

Passos Atuais
STEPS FOR NOW

Viagem por Mundos Sutis
TRAVEL THROUGH SUBTLE WORLDS

Segredos Desvelados – *Iberah e Anu Tea*
UNVEILED SECRETS – *Iberah and Anu Tea*

A Criação – *Nos Caminhos da Energia*
CREATION – *On the Paths of Energy*

The Mystery of the Cross In the Present Planetary Transition
O MISTÉRIO DA CRUZ NA ATUAL TRANSIÇÃO PLANETÁRIA

O Nascimento da Humanidade Futura
THE BIRTH OF THE FUTURE HUMANITY

1993

Aos Que Despertam
TO THOSE WHO AWAKEN

Paz Interna em Tempos Críticos
INNER PEACE IN CRITICAL TIMES

A Formação de Curadores
THE FORMATION OF HEALERS

PROFECIAS AOS QUE NÃO TEMEM DIZER SIM
PROPHECIES FOR THOSE WHO ARE NOT AFRAID TO SAY YES

THE VOICE OF AMHAJ
A VOZ DE AMHAJ

O VISITANTE – O CAMINHO PARA ANU TEA
THE VISITOR –*The Way to Anu Tea*

A CURA DA HUMANIDADE
THE HEALING OF HUMANITY

OS NÚMEROS E A VIDAS – *Uma Nova Compreensão da Simbologia Oculta nos Números*
NUMBERS AND LIFE – *A New Understanding of Occult Symbolism in Numbers*

NISKALKAT – *Uma Mensagem para os Tempos de Emergência*
NISKALKAT – *A Message for Times of Emergency*

ENCONTROS COM A PAZ
ENCOUNTERS WITH PEACE

NOVOS ORÁCULOS
NEW ORACLES

UM NOVO IMPULSO ASTROLÓGICO
A NEW ASTROLOGICAL IMPULSE

1994

BASES DO MUNDO ARDENTE – *Indicações para Contato com os Mundos suprafíscicos*

BASES OF THE FIERY WORLD – *Indications for Contacts with Suprafisical Worlds*

CONTATOS COM UM MONASTÉRIO INTERATERRENO
CONTACTS WITH AN INTRATERRESTRIAL MONASTERY

OS OCEANOS TÊM OUVIDOS
OCEANS HAVE EARS

A TRAJETÓRIA DO FOGO
THE PATH OF FIRE

GLOSSÁRIO ESOTÉRICO
ESOTERIC LEXICON

1995

THE LIGHT WITHIN YOU
A LUZ DENTRO DE TI

1996

DOORWAY TO A KINGDOM
PORTAL PARA UM REINO

BEYOND KARMA
ALÉM DO CARMA

1997

WE ARE NOT ALONE
NÃO ESTAMOS SÓS

WINDS OF THE SPIRIT
VENTOS DO ESPÍRITO

FINDING THE TEMPLE
  O ENCONTRO DO TEMPLO

THERE IS PEACE
  A PAZ EXISTE

1998

PATH WITHOUT SHADOWS
  CAMINHO SEM SOMBRAS

MENSAGENS PARA UMA VIDA DE HARMONIA
  MESSAGES FOR A LIFE OF HARMONY

1999

TOQUE DIVINO
  THE DIVINE TOUCH

COLEÇÃO PEDAÇOS DE CÉU
  BITS FROM HEAVEN COLLECTION
- **AROMAS DO ESPAÇO**
  AROMAS FROM SPACE
- **NOVA VIDA BATE À PORTA**
  A NEW LIFE AWAITS YOU
- **MAIS LUZ NO HORIZONTE**
  MORE LIGHT ON THE HORIZON
- **O CAMPANÁRIO CÓSMICO**
  THE COSMIC CAMPANILE
- **NADA NOS FALTA**
  WE LACK NOTHING
- **SAGRADOS MISTÉRIOS**
  SACRED MYSTERIES

- **ILHAS DE SALVAÇÃO**
  ISLANDS OF SALVATION

2002

CALLING HUMANITY
UM CHAMADO ESPECIAL

2004

ÉS VIAJANTE CÓSMICO
YOU ARE A COSMIC WAYFARER

IMPULSOS
IMPULSES

2005

PENSAMENTOS PARA TODO O ANO
THOUGHTS FOR THE WHOLE YEAR

2006

TRABALHO ESPIRITUAL COM A MENTE
SPIRITUAL WORK WITH THE MIND

Published by Editora Irdin
Carmo da Cachoeira, Minas Gerais, Brazil

2009

SIGNS OF BLAVATSKY – *An Unusual Encounter for the Present Time*

SINAIS DE BLAVATSKY – *Um Inusitado Encontro nos Dias de Hoje*

2012

Consciências e Hierarquias
CONSCIOUSNESSES AND HIERARCHIES

2015

Mensagens Reunidas
COLLECTED MESSAGES

Mensagens para Sua Tranformaçã
MESSAGES FOR YOUR TRANSFORMATION

2017

Páginas de Amor e Compreensão
PAGES OF LOVE AND COMPREHENSION

2018

Novos Tempos: Nova Postura
NEW TIMES: NEW ATTITUDE

2020

Versos Livres
OBRA PÓSTUMA

Trigueirinho's works are published by:

Associação Irdin Editora – www.irdin.org.br (selected titles of books in English, Spanish and Portuguese and CDs in several languages), Carmo da Cachoeira, MG, Brazil.

Editora Pensamento – www.pensamento-cultrix.com.br (titles in Portuguese), São Paulo, SP, Brazil

Editorial Kier – www.kier.com.ar (selected titles in Spanish), Buenos Aires, Argentina.

Lichtwelle-Verlag – www.lichtwelle-verlag.ch (selected titles in Spanish and German), Zurich, Switzerland.

Shasti Association – www.shasti.org (selected titles in English), Mount Shasta, CA, USA